THE GOOD ANGEL GUIDE

THE GOOD ANGEL GUIDE

for reluctant sinners

Alix de Saint-André

*Translated from the French
by Elfreda Powell*

SOUVENIR PRESS

First published in France by
NiL éditions, Paris
under the title *Archives des Anges*

This translation first published 1999 by
Souvenir Press Ltd.,
43 Great Russell Street, London WC1B 3PA

ISBN 0 285 63529 8

Typeset by Rowland Phototypesetting Ltd.,
Bury St Edmunds, Suffolk

Printed in Great Britain by
Creative Print and Design Group (Wales), Ebbw Vale

In memory of Bertrand, Laure, Pauline and all
the children who now sing with the angels

On the whole, I would rather people did not
distance themselves from the faith that is part of
their culture, and that they experienced the value
of their own religious tradition.
His Holiness the Dalai Lama

... our God is in the heavens: he hath done
whatsoever he hath pleased.
Psalm cxv

Contents

Acknowledgements

Biblical extracts are taken from the King James version, the most widely known and loved in the UK. However, this book sometimes makes reference to verses not included in it, in which case the reader is referred to the Jerusalem Bible used by the Roman Catholic Church.

Extracts from the Authorized version of The Bible (The King James Bible), the rights in which are vested in the Crown, are reproduced by permission of the Crown's Patentee, Cambridge University Press.

Extracts from The Koran, translated by N.J. Dawood (Penguin Classics 1956, Fifth revised edition 1990) copyright © N. J. Dawood, 1956, 1959, 1966, 1968, 1974, 1990. Reproduced by permission of Penguin Books Ltd., London.

Introduction

In which the author admits she has never seen an angel, but intends to talk about them anyway.

I have never seen an angel in my life. Not even a tiny one. Not a single wing or feather—nothing. Pointless to go on about it.

Anyway, if we were serious we would be discussing something else—like elephants, for example. African grey or Asian in their festive regalia, ivory white or even alcoholic pink: everyone knows what an elephant is. Nothing could be harder to mistake for something else. Put a trunk in front, a tail behind, and four feet in between—add a couple of tusks and you have an elephant. More or less. It would be difficult to write anything silly about elephants—that they have eight feet, for instance—unless you were having a giggle with a small child. But when it comes to angels . . . If you said that a seraph had twelve wings, it would be quite a big fib, and it would risk falling completely flat because far too many people do not know that a seraph has six wings. And many more—and who can blame them?—don't even know what a seraph is, for the simple reason that they have never seen one.

And that is as good a reason as any.

The annoying thing is that angels are invisible. If they were parked in the sky like elephants in a zoo, we might be able to see them through a giant telescope; they could be photographed by satellite, with their swords and trumpets, surfing an anticyclone in the Azores; but, alas, the weathergirl with the nice boobs is unlikely ever to interrupt her flow to make jokes about seraphim.

*

11

Suddenly the doors to the realms of moonshine are open wide and this investigation into angels is on the road. There are any number of practical manuals around that claim to give the names of experts you can call to deal with mildew or hay fever; and you can find others that will give you a magic formula for activating your guardian angel during an ambush or when you run into thick fog on the motorway. If they are to be believed, angels combine the properties of a mobile, a personal lightning conductor, a pet and Tinker Bell. So why be without one? Give up the Prozac now and adopt an angel, or even several: there's no danger of them peeing on the carpet. With these heavenly accessories you can live a risk-free spiritual life. And they can be delivered just in time to calm any metaphysical anguish the millennium might bring.

This is cloud-cuckoo land.

The writers of this distressing angel pornography have the nerve to assume that we have the right to put these invisible strangers into orbit around our fascinating navels so as to transform them, on the spot, into instruments of our pleasure or intellectual comfort. Wouldn't both they and we benefit from a closer knowledge?

For angels—if they exist—are not things, but living beings. And as such they at least merit the same caring attention that we give to plants and animals. If they don't exist, they are still part of our heritage, and amongst the most beautiful images of humanity's great dream. They should not be used in such grotesque fashion.

So what are they? How can one really find out about angels? Where is this heavenly community's information bureau?

Science is of no great assistance here, since science depends on observation, and a characteristic of angels, as everyone will vouch, is that they avoid being observed. Even if quantum physics has proved the existence of unobservable phenomena that are nonetheless real, the word 'angel' has not yet entered its vocabulary.

Nor can philosophy help, for it is concerned with ideas, and angels are not ideas. Many philosophers recognise that there could exist, midway between human and divine, another category of beings; some have even classified them, under the name of 'eons'. But when it comes to pronouncing on their lifestyle, even Descartes,[1] who believed in the existence of angels, felt it quite beyond his sphere of competence to talk about them. They were off his beat. Philosophers say: angels are a matter of theology, not philosophy—so go and ask God about them!

God? Yes, the very same, in the singular. The one and only true God. At a time when it is highly fashionable to be Buddhist we have to admit that, all on His own like that, He appears offputting. However, in traditional cultures that are swarming with gods, angels do not exist as such. That's how it is. And if one starts mixing up the gods on Olympus with feathered demigods, avatars of Vishnu and other sophisticated reincarnations of Buddha, one very quickly runs the risk of confusing angels with any old winged entity, perhaps even beings in disguise—because they can be practical jokers too . . . —if those amiable creatures up there in the archaic or exotic heavens will forgive us for saying so.

Of course, no one is obliged to believe in God, but when it comes to angels you have to go along with Him, because without God the idea of angels is absurd—they would be flying in a vacuum. In order for an angel to take off with his wings at full spread and to complete his trajectory, God has to be there on the runway and man has to be at touchdown point. There is no avoiding that.

And so, to begin at the beginning . . .

'The Lord God formed man of the dust of the ground, and breathed into his nostrils the breath of life; and man became a living soul.'[2] This is the way our biblical adventures begin. Brought to life out of mud—that's what we are. In Hebrew man is *adam* and earth *adama*: man is literally an earthling, made of earth. In English, too, 'human' and 'humus' have the same root—as does 'humility'—which seems a good starting-point for a study of angels. We must keep our feet firmly on the ground—a tiny anchorage in the vast universe. Earthbound through gravity, man is a heavy being. But an angel is extraterrestrial. Neither earthling nor made of earth, he is

---

1 René Descartes, French Rationalist philosopher, 1596–1650.
2 Genesis ii, 7

not even as light as a feather—he weighs nothing, he exerts no pressure, he has no weight.

The word angel comes from *aggelos*, a Greek translation of the Hebrew *malakh*, meaning 'messenger'. No more, no less. We do not know what an angel is made of, we only know what he does: an angel is a being that moves. In punctuation terms he is a dash. So how do we go about establishing the identity of a being of no fixed abode, with no size, weight, sex or age—nothing except a profession?

Although we have an address for God, we have not got much further. A case in point is an ingenious American who recounted his angelic misadventures in the *Los Angeles Times*. Full of goodwill and energy, one day towards the end of the 1950s he set off in search of the angels in the Bible. Only years later—at the height of the hippie era—did he return from his long and very perplexing journey. He had, of course, seen any number of angels—often 'too much', sometimes 'scary'. But what were they made of? What was their history? When had they been created? Anybody's guess. From his great expedition he had brought back only the names of Michael, Gabriel and Raphael, three out of the seven archangels. So what about the other four? Having skipped not a single page, he concluded bitterly that the Bible was the last place to look for information on angels.

Had he read the Koran—an idea that crosses very few Americans' minds—our adventurer would have reached the same point, give or take a name or two: the Scriptures that merit a capital letter (the Bible, the Gospels, the Koran)—all starring God—recount the story of what has happened between God and mankind. Throughout these turbulent sagas the angels, formidable though they may be, are secondary characters, mere doers of errands. They play the same thankless role as confidants in classical drama—that of messenger, as their name indicates. And the Scriptures are more interested in the message itself, in its Divine Sender and in its human destination than in the errand boy, however pretty he may be—which is always the case with angels in so far as they are allowed to be glimpsed at all.

Angels are agents of heaven's Telecom. But the Bible is not a directory.

What is more, the world has never been short of pernickety rabbis, bishops and mufti all too ready to put those dreamy children of Abraham on their guard against a potential passion for angels. That there should be only one God was quite enough to take, for a start—but at least one knew to Whom one should address one's prayers. Any disloyal competition had to be stopped. The cult of angels could have led to worse: idolatry, heresy, even Satanism—the worst of the worst—because in the community of angels the most seductive are not necessarily the good ones. So beware!

No longer do such threats make us smile, now that we see news items showing the chilling figures of pale adolescents engaged, every full moon, in digging up the poor dead. Satan, too, is an angel.

At this stage, perhaps the seeker after angels should abandon his or her inquiry. Certainly not! Because, thank God, even if the leaders of our three traditions—Judaism, Christianity and Islam—have always taught us to worship only God, they have never forbidden an *interest* in angels. And so for centuries people have annotated the Sacred Books with regard to these very mysterious characters. Few texts have been so closely read, intoned, commented upon and argued over as these. And it is in their margins that gradually, over the years, the history of angels has come to be written. Speculating and discussing, the sages, saints and storytellers have continued to weave their angelologies, full of wisdom and poetry—humour, too. And each of these Scriptures has thus given birth to a host of little books that echo a lively and uninterrupted oral tradition.

From this mass of documents each of us knows, at best, only scraps. It is unlikely—and perhaps only the least neurotic of us could cope with it—that all three traditions should be inherited within a single family; schools rarely teach the history of religions, and believers themselves (in spite of orders from Above) often put far more zeal into tearing each other to bits than into admitting that they are quarrelling over the same God and very often the same angels.

Today, when an ill wind blows these misunderstood beings towards a new and pretty polluted peak of popularity, plunging into the archives to find their true origins comes like a breath of fresh air. Up until now, angels have been the only extraterrestrials ever seen on this planet; and since accounts of their visitations exist, it would be short-sighted not to consult them.

Of course, those who have written such accounts are not policemen; without seeing in their approach the slightest contradiction, they combine a sense of wonder with concern for the truth. They view their lives in the light of another world of which these strange travellers are witnesses—and as real in their eyes as the noisiest of grey elephants. And while they greatly fear them, they sometimes refer to them with a gentle familiarity as 'our older brothers, the angels'.

This book is but a tiny rediscovered fragment of a vast heritage of fellowship. What follows are some true stories about angels. Nothing has been invented here—or perhaps everything has.

Chapter One

Revelations

In which we learn of the circumstances of Jacob's, Mary's and later Mohammed's encounters with angels, and of the consequences for all mankind; discover the ensuing links between Jews, Christians and Muslims, as well as their reasons for squabbling; and state with great satisfaction that the angels are common to all three, and not, in fact, a subject for dispute.

Let us begin at the beginning—with God.

God's defining characteristic is that He speaks. It matters little whether we call Him Jehovah,[1] God the Father, or Allah. It amounts to the same thing: there is only one of Him. He is invisible—'for there shall no man see me, and live'[2]—but he can talk.

He did not create the world with His hands but with words. 'And God said, Let there be light: and there was light.'[3] Such divine simplicity: there is no difference between what He says and what is. All He has to do is speak, and speak He does. When He delivered the Ten Commandments on Mount Sinai, He was heard but not seen, as Moses would later recall: 'And the Lord spake unto you out of the midst of the fire: ye heard the voice of the words, but saw no similitude; only ye heard a voice.'[4]

So if you want to discover God, you must lend an ear.

1 Translators' vocalisation of the Hebrew name for God, YHVH—'He who should not be mentioned in vain'. Several meanings exist, including 'He who was, is and shall be'.
2 Exodus xxxiii, 20.
3 Genesis i, 3.
4 Deuteronomy iv, 12.

The Shema, the prayer that every observant Jew recites morning and evening as an affirmation of the Jewish faith, begins with 'Hear, O Israel: the Lord our God is one Lord.' *Shema* means 'Listen'. *Ausculta, o fili!*—'Listen, my son'— are the first words, in Latin, of the rule of Saint Benedict which orders silence in all its monasteries throughout Christian Europe, because according to the first words of St John's Gospel: 'In the beginning was the Word, and the Word was with God, and the Word was God.'

Why does God reveal himself through our sense of hearing? Perhaps because it is the most far-reaching of the five: we can only see what is in front of us, for example, whereas we can hear all around us—and God is everywhere.

It soon transpires that this talking God's overriding concern is to make Himself heard by people, who often find that they have more pressing things to attend to. In order to do this—and to avoid fatal heart attacks which too direct an intervention on His part might well provoke—He often resorts to a visible angel as intermediary, who assumes, for the occasion, human (exclusively male) form. And these angel-messengers are always such handsome young men that, had they had wings (this type of angel never wears them when on duty), they might have left a few feathers around in Sodom: in fact, the Sodomites found them so sexy that they would quite willingly have raped them, had not Lot offered them protection in his house.[1]

Before we turn to some of the not-so-famous angels, let us pause and take in some of the stars, those angels whose messages were fundamental to Judaism, Christianity and Islam—to cite them in their order of appearance on our planet. At the very beginning of each of the three monotheisms there was a revelation: a meeting with an angel, which is always a meeting with God.

And as a rule it takes two to play.

1 Genesis xix, 1–5.

A STRANGE WRESTLER

Jacob saw angels on several occasions. He was not the first to do so, and, in his family at least, no one was surprised by it. On the other hand, he remains the first man in the Bible to have a set-to with an angel. People still talk about it—for as a result of this nocturnal scuffle, which took place around 1700 BC, Jacob earned a name which still resounds today: the name of Israel.

Jacob was an odd type. His grandfather Abraham was the first man to whom God had spoken since the flood, and He had promised him descendants as numerous as the stars of heaven. His father Isaac, who had escaped being sacrificed, preferred Esau (his elder brother by a whisker—they were twins) to him, but Jacob was the darling of his mother Rebekah. A very handsome lad, he was soft and smooth, and his face, so they said, would be imparted to the crescent moon. Esau was a redhead, and hairy all over like a fur coat, according to the story in Genesis, the first Book of the Bible.

While the comely Jacob hung around his mother's skirts in camp, Esau used to spend his time hunting on the plains, and would arrive home ravenous. And so it was that his cheeky brother Jacob took advantage one day and swapped Esau's birthright for a bowl of steaming lentils. He had lost his birthright for a mess of potage, as the saying goes—which he, alas, could not have known at the time because it would derive from his misadventures. For Jacob it was a good day's work. However, in order to be truly the eldest, in not just a material but a spiritual sense, Jacob still had to obtain his father's blessing. As he had got older Isaac had gone blind, and this gave his mother Rebekah an idea. Using her talents as a dressmaker, she disguised her hairless son as his hairy elder brother by making him a handsome goatskin shirt. The ruse worked: in the half-light of his father's tent, Jacob pretended to be Esau—whom Isaac thought he recognised as he felt Jacob's fake fur, and he blessed him as his elder son. When Esau came home from the hunt, it was too late.

Esau 'cried with a great and exceeding bitter cry', the

Scriptures say.[1] 'Is not he rightly named Jacob? for he hath supplanted me these two times: he took away my birthright; and, behold, now he hath taken away my blessing.' He was, of course, quite right to be on his guard: in Hebrew Jacob means 'usurper'.[2]

But a blessing, even a usurped one, cannot be withdrawn.

As the big hairy Esau, mightily enraged, threatened to kill his scoundrel of a brother, Rebekah, until such time as Esau should calm down, sent her dear little Jacob far away to her own family to look for a wife. Many years later and after numerous adventures, with his fortune made, more wives than he could ever have dreamed of and already the father of eleven children, Jacob came home, ready at last to confront his brother Esau. That night he spent alone—or perhaps not. This is what the Scriptures say:

> And . . . there wrestled a man with him until the breaking of the day. And when he saw that he prevailed not against him, he touched the hollow of his thigh; and the hollow of Jacob's thigh was out of joint, as he wrestled with him.
>
> And he said, Let me go, for the day breaketh. And he said, I will not let thee go, except thou bless me.
>
> And he said unto him, What is thy name? And he said, Jacob.
>
> And he said, Thy name shall be called no more Jacob, but Israel, for as a prince hast thou power with God and with men, and hast prevailed.
>
> And Jacob asked him, and said, Tell me, I pray thee, thy name. And he said, Wherefore is it that thou dost ask after my name? And he blessed him there.[3]

Apparently, the poor American we mentioned earlier was quite miffed that this unknown 'man', who turned out to be an angel, should preserve his anonymity by not telling Jacob his name. However, to continue.

The important thing was that, in a keen fight, Jacob had

1 Genesis xxvii, 34.
2 Genesis xxvii, 36. The name comes from *aqav*, 'to supplant'.
3 Genesis xxxii, 24–9.

obtained the ultimate blessing, the blessing of God, which would make him the true elder son, the spiritual heir to Abraham and to God's promise. Esau, who had taken three Hittite wives—'a grief of mind unto Isaac and to Rebekah'[1]— would be father to the Edomites, the 'descendants of the redhead,'[2] whom no one cared about, whereas Jacob's twelve sons would be the fathers of the twelve tribes of Israel, the Israelites.

And yet God knew that Jacob was a usurper: He can see everything, even in the dark ... And then you have to consider what a cheek Jacob had, wrestling with an angel! When you see an angel, you're supposed to grovel. And why was the angel of God less strong than Jacob?

None of this corresponds to the accepted idea of how one goes about obtaining God's blessings, and, even less, of the way angels behave in society. How is it conceivable that such heavenly personages can come to earth and fight like tom cats, not even respecting the Queensberry rules?

For this angel—certainly no gentleman—had some odd manners. To get the upper hand he played dirty, hit Jacob below the belt—literally. What we are talking about here is the sciatic nerve, and what the Bible prudishly refers to as 'touching the hollow of his thigh' is nothing less than a punch in the goolies ... and one so violent that Jacob, now Israel, would limp for the rest of his life—for the rest of his 147 years! Thank God, the trauma did not affect his virility— Benjamin, his twelfth son, was born some time after this set-to.

Jacob, frankly, had been asking for it. This was the tribute he had to pay for his tribes. And the angel had not chosen his target at random: you could say it was a sort of muscular blessing that touched Jacob at the very root. After all, the sign of the alliance between God and Abraham is circumcision—and that, too, takes place in a curious spot.

The interesting thing is Jacob's change of identity. The angel gave him, the usurper, a name which would be the

---

1 Genesis xxvi, 35.
2 *Edom* means 'red' in Hebrew.

foundation of Israel. God had promised Abraham that he would be the father of an immense people, and then his grandson Jacob, and this people, God's elect, acquire a name chosen by God himself, a name that means 'he who has prevailed with God'—which is original.

But God is not at all conventional. He can even be quite disconcerting. In Jacob He chose an individual who would resist Him and want His blessing so badly that he would force His hand, as equal to equal. With Jacob, God embarked upon an amorous combat in which He agreed never to have the last word—otherwise, He would have sent him a stronger angel, the sort who destroy whole towns with the flap of a wing. Here, by contrast, He seems to have been holding back, rather like a father boxing with his small son—right up until the end, or nearly.

One wonders what God would have made of Esau, whose hairy chest has since been found by rabbinical commentaries to have no end of creepie-crawlies, but whose least wrongdoing was to have allowed himself to be governed by the rumbling of his belly.

God spurns the half-hearted, and Jacob was not half-hearted. He was a younger son, and God has an undeniable weakness for younger sons and for the last born: Abel was the younger brother of Cain; Isaac, the younger brother of Ishmael; Jacob, the younger brother of Esau; Ephraim, the younger brother of Manassah; then there was Joseph, and Benjamin the well beloved . . . Is it because younger sons are more vulnerable, or less attached to the material things that preoccupy their elder brothers? We shall see. But don't think for a moment that God doesn't like redheads: King David had flaming red hair.

Israel was God's first love, and their alliance endures. Despite the reports of adultery, of estrangements and reconciliations that have gone on since biblical times, this couple have never really grown tired of one another, old as they now are. To please His beloved, Israel has followed a kosher diet for over four thousand years and has never stopped reading the Torah, which is both his marriage contract and the diary of a stormy honeymoon: 'You remember when . . .' Every word He has ever uttered is endlessly commented upon, weighed up and analysed . . . that is, when they are not arguing about who has put what where.

Christians speak of God the Father as the 'God of Abraham, Isaac and Jacob', and this biblical scene of 'wrestling with the angel' has often been depicted in churches. To take a fashionably situated example: Delacroix's painting in Saint-Sulpice in Paris. Jacob can also be found in the Koran, under his two names of Jacob (Ya'qūb in Arabic) and Israel, but there is no mention of the episode where he fights with the angel; this is considered totally implausible by Muslims, who hold that angels behave impeccably.

One small point: what we call the Bible is, etymologically, a library; Jews refer to it as the *TaNaKh*. T stands for Torah, the Law,[1] which consists of the five books attributed to Moses—Genesis, Exodus, Leviticus, Numbers and Deuteronomy—known to Christians as the Pentateuch. N stands for *Nevi'im*: the prophets—Joshua, Judges, Samuel, Kings, Isaiah, Jeremiah, Ezekiel, plus the minor prophets. K stands for *Ketuvim*: the Scriptures—Psalms, Lamentations, Song of Songs, and so on. The Christians' Bible is made up of the Tanakh, which they call the Old Testament, and the New—that is, the texts about Jesus—the four Gospels, the Acts of the Apostles, twenty-one Epistles and the Revelation of St John (also known as the Apocalypse).

Another point: the word 'testament' has two meanings: it comes from the Latin *testamentum*, which in turn is a translation of both the Greek *diathēkē* (meaning 'covenant' and 'clauses or provisions of a will') and the Hebrew *berit* (meaning 'covenant'). Contemporary translators often find it, then, more correct to talk about the First and Second Covenant rather than the Old and New Testament. *Testamentum* derives from the Latin *testis*, meaning both 'witness' and 'testicle', the witness being the person who puts his own attributes in the scales to confirm his evidence. This crude custom was also practised by the patriarchs. Abraham, to make his servant swear on oath, made him 'put his hand

---

1 The usual translation. 'Teachings' would be more accurate: the word's Hebrew root is *yrh*, meaning 'to teach'.

under the thigh'[1]—which is not so far from what happened to Jacob. As soon as the subject of angels arises, it is difficult to avoid the question of sex.

CHRISTMAS GREETINGS

An angel and a woman: everyone knows the tale. We no longer attempt to explain the holy Virgin, or Gabriel either. Without their exchange, there would have been no Jesus. The scene ought to have taken place in the year 1 BC, except that modern historians think that Jesus Christ was born in the year 6 before himself—the calendar was not established until six centuries later by an Armenian monk who made a mistake in his calculations.

Saint Luke recounts the meeting in his Gospel:[2]

The angel Gabriel was sent from God unto a city of Galilee, named Nazareth,

To a virgin espoused to a man whose name was Joseph, of the house of David; and the virgin's name was Mary.

And the angel came in unto her, and said, Hail, thou that art highly favoured, the Lord is with thee: blessed art thou among women.

And when she saw him, she was troubled at his saying, and cast in her mind what manner of salutation this should be.

And the angel said unto her, Fear not, Mary: for thou hast found favour with God.

And, behold, thou shalt conceive in thy womb, and bring forth a son, and shalt call his name JESUS.

He shall be great, and shall be called the Son of the Highest: and the Lord God shall give unto him the throne of his father David:

And he shall reign over the house of Jacob for ever; and of his kingdom there shall be no end.

1 Genesis xxiv, 9.
2 Luke i, 26–38.

Then said Mary unto the angel, How shall this be, seeing I know not a man?

And the angel answered and said unto her, The Holy Ghost shall come upon thee, and the power of the Highest shall overshadow thee: therefore also that holy thing which shall be born of thee shall be called the Son of God.

And, behold, thy cousin Elisabeth, she hath also conceived a son in her old age: and this is the sixth month with her, who was called barren.

For with God nothing shall be impossible.

And Mary said, Behold the handmaid of the Lord; be it unto me according to thy word. And the angel departed from her.

Here the angel Gabriel, with exquisite politeness, plays a very classic role for a biblical angel: he makes known a cardinally important—and improbable—birth. It was also angels who came to announce to Abraham that Sarah, his wife, was going to have a son. And when Sarah, who had heard everything behind the canvas of her tent, had burst out laughing (she was ninety and Abraham was almost a hundred), one of the angels, shocked by her reaction, had replied in similar vein to her: 'Is any thing too hard for the Lord?'[1] Quite naturally, if one can use that phrase, their son Isaac was born within the year.

What is new in Luke's story is the proposal of marriage. To which the young Mary replies with the practicality that she will always demonstrate: at the marriage feast in Cana, for example, it was she who pointed out that they were beginning to run out of wine, thereby inaugurating her son's miraculous career. When Mary protested to the angel that she had never known a man, even though she was betrothed, what she really meant was that she was a virgin. This is the famous 'to know in the biblical sense', one of the most popular euphemisms ever.

Christianity was born of this meeting of words between an angel and a maiden. According to a medieval apocryphal

1 Genesis xviii, 9–14.

gospel, 'The Word of God entered her through her ear, and thus it was that the pregnancy of the Virgin Mary began'; this was to be the only case ever of auricular insemination. On a more serious note Mary's reply to the angel, '*Fiat!*'[1]— in Latin 'So be it', reminiscent of the initial divine *Fiat lux!*, the first words pronounced by God in the Bible, meaning 'Let there be light!'—would redeem mankind, corrupted by Eve's collaboration with the Devil.

The very first time that an angel spoke to a woman had left some pretty bad memories: the angel was Satan, the wicked angel, the serpent who had persuaded Eve in the Garden of Eden to take a bite of the forbidden fruit, with all the disastrous consequences that this act had engendered for her descendants — painful childbirth, women's submission to their husbands, travail and death, and other jollities.[2] In the Middle Ages there was this famous anagram: Eva ('Eve' in Latin), in reverse, is *Ave* ('Hail'), the angel's greeting to Mary. So Mary is Eve in reverse. Even today there are numerous statues showing Mary trampling with her naked feet the snake which so fascinated Eve.

This 'Ave Maria'—'Hail, Mary'—that Gabriel uttered is now one of the best known, oldest, most repeated prayers in the Catholic Church: fifty-three times per chaplet and 153 times per rosary. As for the angel, his name lives on in the angelus, a prayer which first appeared in the twelfth century, immortalised in a painting by Millet,[3] which was then popularised on a French post office calendar. This prayer, recited morning, noon and evening to the sound of bells since the fifteenth century, also contains three *Ave*s, and it owes its title, as do all prayers, to its first word, *Angelus Domini nuntiavit Mariae*, meaning 'The Angel of the Lord announced unto Mary.'

While Mary has only a very discreet presence in the Gospels themselves, in most Christian religions she is of immense importance, for many reasons. In fact, with Christianity God exploded in three dimensions. And Mary was the fuse to this

---

1 *Fiat mihi secundum verbum tuum*: 'As it is according to thy word'.
2 Genesis iii, 14–19.
3 The nineteenth-century artist Jean-François Millet.

Jesus. They have filled your brain and the very marrow of your bones to bursting point with it, so that your mind has come to believe in it. And yet common sense cannot accept it ... That the Creator of heaven and earth, and all that is within them, should enter into the womb of a Jewish woman and wait nine months, let her give birth to a baby, who grows up and is then delivered into the hands of his enemies, who judge him, condemn him to death and kill him, and that finally he should be restored to life again and return to his first abode—all this is intolerable to the minds of all Jews as it is to all men!

On the other hand, paradoxically, the miraculous birth of Jesus poses no problems for Muslims. Christians tend to be ignorant of the position Mary holds under the name of Maryam in the Koran, which has a lot more to say about her than have the Gospels. The third sura[1] recounts her genealogy, tells of her father Joachim (Imrān), her cousin Elisabeth (Ishba), her birth, her adolescence in the Temple with her Uncle Zacharias and even the angel Gabriel's visitation near the wells of Salwān, announcing the future miraculous birth of Jesus (Issa):

The angels[2] said to Mary: 'God bids you rejoice in a Word from Him. His name is the Messiah, Jesus son of Mary. He shall be noble in this world and in the world to come, and shall be one of those who are favoured. He shall preach to men in his cradle and in the prime of manhood, and shall lead a righteous life.'[3]

The astonishment of the young girl appears in another chapter: '"How shall I bear a child," she answered, "when I have neither been touched by any man nor ever been unchaste?"'[4] The spirit of God entered Mary through 'the

---

1 Any section of the Koran.
2 'Gabriel is usually designated by the plural form,' notes Sheikh Si Hanza Boubakeur in his French translation of the Koran, Maisonneuve & Larose.
3 Koran iii, 45–6.
4 Koran xix, 20.

slit in her gown', according to Koranic tradition, which also says that all children cry at birth because they are stung by Satan. All except two—Mary and Jesus.

Muslims believe Mary to be the virgin mother of the prophet Jesus, prophet of the ultimate prophet, Mohammed. They call Jesus 'the Anointed One', which has the same meaning as the Hebrew *Maschiah*, Messiah, or *Khristos*, Christ, in Greek: 'he who has received divine unction'. But Muslims consider Jesus to be neither God nor the son of God. That, for them, would be blasphemous. God has no associates and no children. 'He begot none, nor was He begotten.'[1] And since, according to Muslims, Jesus was not crucified, neither did he rise from the dead. Someone else was crucified in his stead, and the living Jesus ascended directly into heaven, whence he will return at the end of time. That for them seems more honourable—crucifixion was in fact an infamous punishment—and much more rational.

THE READING LESSON

Born on 1 September AD 570 in Mecca and orphaned at a tender age, Mohammed did not have a very happy childhood. Carted around from one person to another, he was finally taken in by a caravaneer uncle. His youth was divided between Syria and Palestine, where he met Jews and Christians; and part of that time he spent fighting alongside his clan. At twenty-five he entered the service of a rich widow, Khadija, whom he married some time later and by whom he had four daughters. He had everything to make him happy when, at about the age of forty, he passed through a critical period of solitary meditation. Tormented by anguish, all alone and fasting, he would go for longer and longer retreats to a cave on Mount Hira. At night he was racked by nightmares: it seemed to him that a being 'as huge as the distance between Earth and heaven' appeared to him and wanted to take hold of him. He would wake up sweating and trembling all over. By day he wandered, dishevelled and emaciated, believing himself to be mad or possessed—until one evening

1 Koran cxii, 2–3.

in the last week of the month of Ramadan in the year 612, which Muslims call 'the night of destiny', the night on which the angel Gabriel spoke to him.

> The angel came to me while I slept. In his hand he held a piece of embroidered cloth which contained a book.
> 'Read!' he ordered me.
> 'But I can't read,' I replied.
> Then he pressed the book against my mouth and my nostrils so forcefully that I was about to suffocate. For a moment I thought that he was death itself. Then he let me go.[1]

The angel repeated his command and his harsh gesture twice. After the third time Mohammed asked him what he should read, and the angel said some words to him that Mohammed repeated and inscribed in his heart. Then the angel disappeared, and Mohammed awoke and left the cave.

> Hardly had I reached halfway down the mountain when I heard a voice saying, 'O Mohammed! You are the apostle of Allah and I am Gabriel.' I raised my head and looked towards the sky, and there indeed was Gabriel, in the guise of a man, his feet touching the horizon. He spoke to me once more: 'O Mohammed. You are the apostle of Allah, and I am Gabriel.' I stopped and looked at him, unable to move either forward or back. Then I began to turn my face towards the other points on the horizon, but there was nowhere in the sky that I could look without seeing the angel in the same stance. And so I remained standing, unable either to advance or to retrace my steps.

It was not until the next day, at nightfall, that Mohammed returned home. For more than twenty years he would proclaim the Book that was engraved on his heart, and in which

---

1 A traditional story, 'The Birth of Islam', told by Toufic Fahd in *Histoire des religions* (History of Religions), La Pléiade, Gallimard.

the angel continued to instruct him. Relations between Gabriel and Mohammed, despite their brutal beginning, continued to improve to the point where, one night some ten years later, Gabriel took him off on horseback to visit the heavens.

For Mohammed there was no question but to obey the angel. Gabriel (Jibrīl in Arabic) here regained the vigour of a biblical angel and all but suffocated him, but Mohammed made no move to defend himself; he tried, with all his might, to obey. This is a long way from Jacob the fighter ... *Islam* means 'submission'. Following the prophet, Muslims want to submit to God—to be slaves, even, according to certain translations.

The first thing that the angel said to Mohammed was 'Read!'—*'Iqra!'* in Arabic—from which comes *Qur'ān*, in English the Koran, 'The Recitation'. There is only a single Scripture, inscribed on the well guarded table (*al-lawh al-mahfūz*) next to God, and which has been handed down through the ages to His prophets: Abraham, Moses, Jesus and Mohammed. Muslims consider, then, that Jews and Christians are, like them, 'people of the Book'. But this Book is in heaven. *'Mektub!'* Muslims repeat—'It is written.' Everything is written. Even the heavenly angels are dipping their pens in the ink and, with God dictating, an angel is writing down man's destiny in his mother's womb, even though he has barely arrived there.

Following the angel Gabriel's command, study is given priority—and not only of the Koran. From the early Middle Ages, Muslim sages were famous in all domains: al-Khwārizmī, who invented algebra around 830, is far from being an isolated example. 'For him who opens a way to seek out knowledge, God shall open a way to paradise. The angels shall submit, with their wings lowered, to please him. All the hosts of the heavens and of the Earth, even the whales of the sea, shall ask pardon of God for him who seeks to learn,' says a hadīth (a remark attributed to the Prophet).

Gabriel's size in Mohammed's final vision is a good indication of the importance of angels in Islam: it is considerable—it is nothing less than an article of faith. Muslims proclaim: 'We believe in God, in his angels, in his Books, in his messengers and in the day of the resurrection.' A Muslim who did not believe in angels would be, quite simply, a renegade.

For Muslims, the Koran is the word of God; Gabriel was simply there to dictate it to Mohammed. There is only one God (Allah), the God of Abraham, of Moses, of Jesus and of Mohammed, His last prophet, whose coming Jesus announced in the Gospel according to Saint John: '. . . if I go not away, the Comforter will not come unto you; but if I depart, I will send him unto you . . . Howbeit when he, the Spirit of truth, is come, he will guide you into all truth; for he shall not speak of himself; but whatsoever he shall hear, that shall he speak; and he will shew you things to come.'[1] Christians understand this Comforter—or Paraclete, from the Greek *paraklētos*, 'counsellor', 'consoler'[2]—to be the Holy Spirit who would come down to the apostles at Pentecost. For Muslims, read the Greek word *paraklytos*, which means 'worthy of being praised'—in Arabic, *muhammad*, from which Mohammed.

Muslims recognise the validity of the Bible and the Gospels, with the proviso that in their opinion, since these texts were edited long after the events in question, Jews and Christians have tampered with them a very great deal. So just as Jesus is neither God nor the son of God, neither are the Israelites in any way the chosen people, nor did God ever make any covenant with them; equally, Abraham did not lead away his son Isaac (whom he had by his wife Sarah, and who was father of Jacob and ancestor of the Jews) to be sacrificed, but rather his eldest son Ishmael (born of an Egyptian servant called Agar, and ancestor of the Arabs), and so on.

Only the Koran can re-establish the truth. In the same way that Christianity believes itself to be the culmination of Judaism, so Islam considers itself to be the supreme culmination of the two monotheisms that preceded it.

Clearly, neither the Jews nor the Christians understand it in the same way. For them, Mohammed is not a prophet: he is quite simply an inspired man, a warrior, and, in the way

1 John xvi, 7–13.
2 The Gospels were written in Greek.

of patriarchs, polygamous.[1] He established a simple, absolute and universal monotheism for his people, who had until then been pagans. In order to do this he used what he had learnt through his encounters. First he adapted and simplified Judaism: in the Muslim Sharia can be found the Jewish Halakhah, a law which regulates every minute and every aspect of the believer's life; also to be found—under the same name, even—is the Tahāra, embodying the principles of purity and impurity, eating taboos and so forth. To this revisited Judaism Mohammed would have added Arianism, a very widespread Christian heresy of his period—to be condemned in 325 at the Council of Nicea—which did not recognise Christ's divinity.

From all these divergencies, however, there emerged a smaller—but infinitely great—common denominator: no one doubted the existence of the one God.

Each one of the monotheisms is equally sure about its descent from Abraham: the legitimate grandfather (via Jacob) of the Jews, the natural grandfather (via Ishmael) of the Muslims, and the adoptive grandfather (via Mary) of the Christians. This descent today represents half the world's population and earns Abraham the unassailable title of 'father of believers'. Nor does any of the three contest either the existence or the power of the angel Gabriel.

---

1 He had ten wives: Khadija, Sauda, 'A'icha, Hafsa, Umm Salāma, Zaynab, Safiyya, Jowayriya, Umm Habība and Maymūna, as well as several concubines.

Chapter Two

Investigations

In which we answer some basic questions about angels—how old are they? how many are there? what language do they speak? what do they eat?; indicate how all this information has been collected and verified; and strive to calculate God's size and other marvels.

How would we answer a cub reporter's questions about angels—When? How? What? How many? Why?—without saying just a load of twaddle? We could attempt a line-by-line reading of the Scriptures, as did the courageous American we mentioned earlier, but that would not get us very far. Commentators over the centuries have therefore resorted to other methods. Sometimes they have lifted each verse, each word and even each letter and sounded them like pebbles against others from elsewhere in the text, watching for sparks of meaning to leap out and set the imagination alight. Or perhaps, like gold-washers, they have panned the sand of the chapters with the waters of tradition so as to filter out a myriad interpretations, be they literal, historical or symbolic, in the hope that at the final sifting a brilliant nugget of mystical meaning will shine out.

WHEN WERE THE ANGELS CREATED?

Saint Augustine wrote, 'Nowhere in the accounts of the world given in the Holy Scriptures is there to be found any substantiated reference to the act and order of creation of the angels.'

Indeed. The Bible opens with an ordered account of the creation of the world in six days, in which there is not a trace

35

of angels, not even the tiniest heavenly feather. But shortly after this, angels are there. That they were not created is completely impossible, since nothing, nobody, exists that was not created by God. So *when* were they created? Here is a wonderful subject for our theological Sherlock Holmeses to tear their hair out about, using clues hidden in the sacred verses.

Before the beginning?

'In the beginning God created the heavens and the earth,' says the first sentence in the Bible. But a whole learned assembly of ancient Fathers of the Church—Saint Basil, Saint Gregory Nazianzen, Saint Hilary, Saint Jerome, Saint John of Damascus and Origen—thought that the angels existed even before this statement. This is because in the Book of Job God asks him: 'Where wast thou when I laid the foundations of the earth? . . . When the morning stars sang together, and all the sons of God shouted for joy?'[1] Now, in the Bible 'the sons of God'—*Benē Elohim* in Hebrew—does mean 'angels'. So when God created the Earth, angels were already there to applaud him.

While . . .

They were there, then, but how long had they been there? In the sentence 'Where wast thou when I laid the foundations of the earth?', 'when' has the sense of 'while'. And 'while' does not mean 'before', Gregory the Great remarked, quoting Ecclesiasticus: 'He that liveth for ever hath created all things in general'[2]—that is to say, the angelic world and the visible world.

Rupert, a twelfth-century Benedictine abbot living in Cologne and a practical sort of person, remarked that if the heavens had not been created before the angels, they would for a while have had nowhere to live—which is not at all God's style, perfect host that He is. His contemporaries, the

1 Job xxxviii, 4–7.
2 Ecclesiasticus xviii, 1.

rabbis of the *Bahir*, expressed the same idea but metaphorically:

> It can be likened to a king who, wishing to plant a tree, inspects his garden thoroughly in order to find out whether it contains a spring that will make the tree grow. Having found nothing, he says, 'I am going to dig and search for water, and I shall release a spring so that the tree can live.' He digs and finds a spring of running water; after which, he plants the tree, which then grows and bears fruit because its roots are constantly watered by the spring.[1]

God the gardener-king, therefore, created angels after He had created the heavens.

Yes, but when?

For Catholics it was the Fourth Lateran Council—convened to oppose the Albigensian Cathars, who maintained that if the soul, a good thing, was the work of God, material creation, which was evil, was the work of the Devil—that settled the matter with its *Firmiter* decree. This stated that 'from the beginning of time God created, from nothing, all creatures both spiritual and material—that is to say, the angels and the earthly world, followed by humans, who take after both, composed as they are of spirit and of flesh'. The angels would therefore have been created at the same time as the universe and before mankind.

This is all very well, but somewhat vague: which day between the first and the fifth was it, given that mankind arrived on the sixth? Each day has its advocates and its detractors.

---

1 The *Bahir* ('The Book of Light'), para. 23; the *Bahir* was an early Jewish cabbalistic work, an anthology of statements attributed to various scholars and sages.

The first day, Sunday

GOD CREATED THE SKY, THE EARTH AND THE LIGHT

For   Cosmas the Syrian (AD 550): Angels were created on the first day, right at the beginning, at the same time as heaven and Earth. Bewildered and in darkness, the angels questioned their origin among themselves until God created light—at which point they were enlightened, recognised God and worshipped Him.

For, but later that day   Saint Augustine: 'God said, "Let there be light", and there was light. It is right to see the creation of the angels in this light, for surely they were made part of the eternal light which is the immutable wisdom of God.'[1]

Against   Rabbi Luliani bar Tabri: 'Nothing angelic was created on the first day. For it is written: "I am the Lord that maketh all things; that stretcheth forth the heavens alone; that spreadeth abroad the earth by myself."'[2]

If angels had been there, they could have given God a helping hand that would have been very damaging to monotheism. For this reason, Judaism generally maintains that the angels were not created on the first day.

The second day, Monday

THE FIRMAMENT SEPARATED THE WATERS

For   Rabbi Yohanan (first century): 'The angels were created on the second day. This is what is written: "O Lord my God, who layeth the beams of his chambers in the waters". It is also written: "O Lord my God, who maketh his angels spirits"'.[3]

---

1 *The City of God*, xi, 2.
2 Isaiah xliv, 24.
3 Psalms civ, 3–4.

For   Rabbi Eliezer takes the same verse and explains it this way:

> On the second day, the Holy One, blessed be He, created the firmament, the angels, the fire of the creatures of flesh and blood and the fire of Gehenna. The angels were created on the second day; when they were sent as messengers of His word they were changed into winds, and when they served in his presence they were transformed into fire, as it is said: '[God] maketh his angels of the winds; his ministers of flaming fire.'[1]

For   Petrus Comestor, or Peter the Glutton, found another reason:

> The work of this second day was good, as it was on the other days, but it does not say, 'God saw that this was good.' The Hebrews record, in fact, that on this day Satanael—that is, the angel that is the Devil, Lucifer—was made. Those who traditionally sing the angels' Mass on Mondays, the second day, in praise of the faithful angels, would seem to prove them right. But some saints report that this was done as a sign: the number 2 has a bad reputation in theology, because it is the first to depart from unity. And since God is unity, he hates the idea of division and discord.[2] This is why the work of the second day is not praised until the third, which is considered to be the day of its completion.

1 In Rabbi Eliezer's quotation of Psalm ciii, 4.
2 Proverbs vi, 19.

The third day, Tuesday

THE EARTH BROUGHT FORTH GRASS, THE TREES YIELDED FRUIT

Against   A Muslim tradition has it that Tuesday was the day on which God created everything dreadful.[1] Hence no angels on this day, since they are perfect.[2]

No one is for, anyway.

The fourth day, Wednesday

THE STARS

For   Muslims say: 'God created the angels on Wednesday, djinns on Thursday and Adam on Friday.'[3]

The fifth day, Thursday

FISH AND FOWL

For   Rabbi Hanina (third century): 'The angels were created on the fifth day, since it is written: "And our feathered friends fly above the earth in the firmament of heaven." And it is also written, with regard to seraphim: "With two wings, each flew."'[4] Since angels have wings, they were created at the same time as birds.

But who knows?

The sixth and seventh days

On the sixth day, Friday, beasts and man were created, and on the seventh, Saturday, God 'rested, and was refreshed'[5]—but Muslims hold that He was not tired at all.

---

1 Tabarī, prominent ninth-century Muslim scholar, in his commentary on the Koran; xxiv, 95.

2 Islam does not generally consider Satan as an angel—see Chapter 4.

3 Tabarī, commentary, I, 83, on the authority of Ibn Anas.

4 'Above . . . stood the seraphims: each one had six wings; with twain he covered his face, and with twain he covered his feet, and with twain he did fly.' Isaiah vi, 2.

5 Exodus xxxi, 17.

In the Koran there is no description of the day-by-day creation of the world, even though it is assumed. 'Yet your Lord is God, who in six days created the heavens and the earth and then ascended the throne, ordaining all things.'[1] But one thing is certain: Allah never takes a rest. This is why the day of rest in Islam is Friday, the day of man's creation, and not Saturday, the *shabbat* (Sabbath) of the Jews, who according to the Third Commandment make the day God rested a holy day. Christians have moved their Sabbath from Saturday to Sunday, the day of Christ's resurrection, of the creation of the world and of the re-creation of mankind.

Today this story of Genesis is often viewed as a gentle tale that may have exploited the naïvety of our grandparents' generation, whose minds were so little attuned to scientific rigour. But it is of no importance. Reading their commentaries, it is noticeable that they never took this text literally, but as the expression of a mystery. Fundamentalists and other 'creationists', our contemporaries, would have seemed to them either idiotic or ignorant. In the first century, Philo of Alexandria 'explained Genesis rather as the Stoics explained Homer: for them the *Iliad* and the *Odyssey* were profound allegories in which the most elevated philosophy was hidden'.[2] Later, when Saint Augustine—who argued that 'the letter kills, and the spirit brings it back to life'[3]—said that angels were created on the first day, he went on to explain that since that day was called 'day one' (*dies unus*) and not 'the first', the second, third and all the rest were not *other* days, but that one day repeated to make up the six or seven.

In the Koran, certain verses recount that the length of one of God's days, by his reckoning, would be a thousand years,[4] and from this Muslims conclude that creation must be seen as a series of six phases, or cycles. Others see it as a metaphor

1 Koran x, 3.
2 Émile Mâle, *L'Art religieux du XIIIe siècle en France* (Religious Art in Thirteenth-century France), iv, ch. 1.
3 Saint Ambrose, quoted by Saint Augustine in his *Confessions*, VI, ch. 4.
4 Koran xxii, 47.

to render accessible some particularly complex abstractions, which take the number 6 as their point of departure, 6 being both the sum (1+2+3) and the product (1×2×3) of the first three numbers.

Even more astonishing is that there is a very early rabbinical evolutionist tradition which explains the origin of evil spirits. According to this they would have descended from the male hyena, after numerous transformations: after seven years the hyena became a bat, then the bat a vampire, the vampire a stinging-nettle, the stinging-nettle a spiny snake, and the spiny snake a demon.[1] This predates Darwin by some fifteen centuries!

Be that as it may, in all three traditions the angel is a spiritual being created before man, which sometimes earns him the title of 'elder brother'.

HOW?

Do angels talk? And, if so, in what language?

Everyone thinks they have the answer. Muslims believe that angels speak Arabic, by virtue of a proposition of the Prophet Mohammed's: 'Love Arabs for three reasons: because I am Arab, because the language of the Koran is Arabic, and because the conversations of those who live in Paradise are in Arabic.'[2] And not only do Islamic angels speak Arabic, they also write in it, as one of their many heavenly duties.

The Jews, as well as the early Christians, of whom Paul was one, thought that angels spoke Hebrew like them—except for the angel Gabriel, who spoke seventy languages.[3] In the Bible the number seventy symbolises the 'nations': that is, the non-Jewish peoples. Gabriel is therefore a perfect polyglot. But he is the only one.

A Jewish tradition which postdates the birth of Christianity appears to offer a more satisfying explanation. It recounts that at the time the Tower of Babel was being built, 'The

---

1 *Baba Kamma*, 16a.
2 Reported by Tabarī.
3 *Hagigah*, 16a.

Holy One, blessed be He, summoned the seventy angels sur-
rounding the throne of glory and He said unto them, "Come,
let us descend and bring together the seventy nations and the
seventy languages." He assigned an angel to each nation, but
Israel chose to follow its own destiny."[1] And so it was that,
with an angel to teach them, each people had their own
writing and language, while the people of Israel kept their
original Hebrew. This would explain why everyone under-
stands angels in their own language. If the archangel Michael
had spoken in Hebrew to Joan of Arc, who couldn't even
read or write French, the Hundred Years War would have
dragged on a good deal longer.

And take heed of what Saint Thomas Aquinas had to say
on the subject: 'Angels do not speak in the true sense of the
word: they merely produce sounds in the air which are similar
to human voices.'[2] Obviously.

THE BREAD OF ANGELS

Do angels eat? And if so, what? Is there anything to have a
nibble on in heaven? Agreed, this question may not be of a
very elevated kind, but it has to be asked, all the same.
Because, once again, there are odd bits scattered throughout
the Holy Scriptures from which we can construct some fine
hypotheses.

When Moses was in the desert, a month and a half after
the exodus from Egypt, his people began to cry out that they
would die of hunger. And God said to Moses, 'Behold, I will
rain bread from heaven for you.'[3] The next day, after the
dew had evaporated, 'behold, upon the face of the wilderness
there lay a small round thing, as small as the hoar frost on
the ground. And when the children of Israel saw it, they said
one to another, It is manna: for they wist not what it was
... it was like coriander seed, white; and the taste of it was
like wafers made with honey.'[4]

In Hebrew *man* means 'what?' The Jews ate 'what?'; they

1 *Chapters of Rabbi* Eliezer, ch. 24.
2 *Summa Theologiae*, Ia, Q. 51, art. 3.
3 Exodus xvi, 4. Also mentioned in Koran ii, 57.
4 Exodus xvi, 14–15, 31.

fed themselves on questions until they arrived in the land of Canaan. In a psalm recalling this episode, manna is defined as the 'corn of heaven' and 'angels' food'.[1]

Was this, then, the food that angels eat?

This is what Rabbi Aqiba thought in the second century. But he was soon floored by Rabbi Ishmael, who retorted that angels do not eat bread because during his forty days on the mountain with God, Moses neither ate nor drank. In the presence of God you are neither hungry nor thirsty. And since angels are in the presence of God, it is logical that they do not eat.

Believers did not have to wait for the advent of positivism to find a natural explanation of the manna mystery. They looked for a natural explanation to the miracle of this bread falling from the sky. In the third century, the monks of Saint Catherine in Sinai explained that manna would have come from cochineal beetles biting into tamarisk twigs to extract their sap (whence the shrub's learned name *Tamarix mannifera*). From this these insects make a sort of honey which, in the cold night of the mountains south of the Negev, runs off the branches and solidifies. In years of heavy rainfall, the Bedouin harvest this substitute honey, which is rich in carbohydrates. They call this *man*, too.

And so the good monks did not throw their habits on to the spiky bushes in vain. For they already realised that the Scriptures, *bis repetita*, offered several levels of interpretation of which the literal sense was the lowest.

But to return to the angels and their snacks. While it may be true that there was no question of the angels *eating* manna, there are, according to tradition, celestial bakers, who make it. It is called 'the bread of angels' because the angels made it, and 'bread of the Strong' because men who ate it became as strong as they were. What is more, after they had digested it they had no need to go to the loo, a most practical bonus in the desert, because 'like angels, they had no use for the anus'.[2]

1 Psalm lxxviii, 24–5.
2 *Exodus Rabbah*, xxv, 3.

At the beginning of time, angels added to their role of bakers those of cooks and sommeliers, for before the Fall 'the angels roasted meat for Adam and poured him wine'.[1] Much later, when Saint James of Alcántara, a poor Franciscan, fell into an ecstatic trance just when he should have been preparing a meal for his brother monks, the angels very kindly arrived to do the cooking for him. Anyone who doubts this can go to the Musée du Louvre, where they can see a painting by Murillo of *The Angels' Kitchen*, illustrating this miracle.

In the Book of Proverbs, at a meal prepared by Wisdom— God's Wisdom—bread and wine were served.[2] For Jews, 'bread signifies the written law, and wine the spoken law, which contain things more precious than all the delicious dishes of the world'.[3] When Jesus, referring to manna, said, 'I am the bread of life: he that cometh to me shall never hunger; and he that believeth on me shall never thirst',[4] he was identifying himself as the living, nourishing word of God: 'the living bread that came down from heaven'. This is why Catholics and members of the Orthodox Church call the consecrated host, which in the Eucharist is the body of Christ in the guise of bread, 'the true bread of the angels'.

But angels, though they may indulge in baking, do not eat, because that would create a real diet problem when they turn up incognito on earth in human form to accomplish some secret divine mission. Witness the angel of God who visited Manoah's sterile wife to announce that she would be mother to a hairy son, the future Samson. On his second visit, as is natural for well brought-up humans, 'Manoah said unto the angel of the Lord, I pray thee, let us detain thee, until we shall have made ready a kid for thee. [Manoah did not know that it was the angel of the Lord. And the angel of the Lord said unto Manoah, Though thou detain me, I will not eat of

---

1 *Sanhedrin*, 59b.
2 Proverbs ix, 5.
3 *Zohar*, III, 271b. The *Zohar*, or *Book of Splendour*, thirteenth-century, is a fundamental work of Jewish mysticism.
4 John vi, 35.

thy bread; and if thou wilt offer a burnt offering,[1] thou must offer it unto the Lord.'[2] And the angel simply disappeared into the sacrificial flames.

This kind of exit from a brutal scene immediately gives the lie to the best of covers. In the same way, the angel of God who, earlier on, had been to see Gideon[3] had set fire with the end of his staff to the sacrifice prepared by him. Angels are composed of fire, and fire consumes fire. According to the description of Saint Justin, who was a contemporary of Rabbi Aqiba, 'Unlike us, angels do not have teeth and jaws; they absorb food as they devour it, like fire devouring fuel.'[4]

However, there is in the Bible a very famous angelic meal which has always posed a problem for commentators. This is the meal offered by Abraham to the three angels who come to visit him on the Plains of Mamre. For Abraham 'took butter, and milk, and the calf which he had dressed, and set it before them; and he stood by them under the tree, and they did eat.'[5] So it is written. Now it is impossible that they did so, because first, angels do not eat, and second, this food, which mixed veal with cow's milk, was not kosher. Even if it was only later that the Law was revealed to Moses, it existed well before, and it is clearly understood in Jewish tradition that the patriarchs, and the angels above all, were already observing it.

But it is equally impossible that the text is lying, so either this 'they' must refer to Abraham and his family, not to the angels, *or* the angels only pretended to eat. Interpreters of the Bible have most often favoured the latter explanation—and depend on it in their construing of a later example, this time concerning Raphael in the Book of Tobit, who avows, 'I did neither eat nor drink, but ye did see a vision.'[6] The angels obviously adopted, somewhat before its time,

---

1 In the Jerusalem Bible this is referred to as a 'holocaust': a sacrifice offered to God in which the victim was burnt. To use this term to describe the extermination of the Jews during the Second World War is a blasphemous aberration, because it presupposes that God favoured it.
2 Judges xiii, 15–16.
3 Judges vi, 20–1.
4 Saint Justin (c.100–c.165), *Dialogue with Trypho*.
5 Genesis xviii, 8.
6 Book of Tobit, xii, 19.

St Ambrose's dictum—'When in Rome, do as the Romans do'—for when on missions to Earth in human form, they do as humans do. According to Philo, such an attitude on their part is both symbolic and polite. St Thomas Aquinas called it 'spiritual manducation'.

In the Koran, the question of this problematic meal finds a radical solution: Abraham brings the angels a roast lamb with no butter or milk—therefore kosher—but 'when he saw their hands being withheld from it, he mistrusted them and was afraid of them'.[1] The fact that they did not eat was a precise indicator to Abraham that his guests were angels. They reassured him immediately: 'Have no fear,' they said. 'It is to the people of Lot that we are sent.' Clearly, it was the people of Sodom who had good reason to be anxious.

Angels in the heavens do not eat. But even so they take sustenance. Following Rabbi Isaac, the rabbis quote the words from a psalm: 'His ministers [were] a flaming fire'.[2] This angelic fire is fed by the flaming splendour of the presence of God, of whom it is written, 'In the light of the face of the king is life.' But not all the angels are so close to God. They do not all live together on the same floor. For those who lodge near the ground floor, 'their food consists of the Torah[3] and of good works accomplished in the world below'; so if the children of Israel were to cease to study the word of God and to do good deeds, these particular angels would be deprived of food.

The *Zohar* (*Book of Splendour*) records the strange life of the angels who flicker on and off. Lodged in the second hall— thus not very high up the scale, given that there are seven halls on high—these angels whose task it is to fight men's evil inclinations

> nourish themselves with the smell and perfume of the world below in order to rise higher and be more luminous. They begin to sing a canticle, but have to break off to resume their flight again, remaining invisible until

1 Koran xi, 69-70.
2 Psalm civ, 4.
3 Or 'Pentateuch': the first five books of the Bible, attributed to Moses.

the children of Israel in turn sing a canticle, which gives them the necessary energy to shine more brightly. When the children of Israel study the Torah, the angels fly up to heaven to bear witness.[1]

It is men's prayer that recharges their batteries.

For Muslims, certainly, their prayer can give angels sustenance: 'Praising [God] is their food, reverencing Him their drink; invoking Him through His beautiful names and His attributes is their favourite occupation, adoring Him their joy.'[2] These angelic dishes even have a name: 'The *tesbih* (praise to God) and the *takdiss* (glory to the holiness of God) are the angels' food.'[3]

Perhaps the exhortation of an eighteenth-century angel is easier for us to understand. When, after a good meal, the Swedish Lutheran Swedenborg saw a shining angel appear, the first words the angel said to him were 'Don't eat so much.'

HOW MANY ANGELS ARE THERE?

Here, too, it is futile to hope to find a definitive answer in the Bible.

According to the most ancient Talmudists, the number of angels is infinite. Each angelic legion is composed of a thousand times a thousand angels—that is, a million—but we do not know how many legions there are. To give an example, on Mount Sinai God appeared with twenty-two thousand legions. 'The chariots of God are twenty thousand, even thousands of angels',[4] so the psalm goes; 'thousand thousands ministered unto him, and ten thousand times ten thousand stood before him';[5] 'and the number of them was ten thousand times ten thousand, and thousands of thousands', according to St John.[6]

Some commentators say there are 496,000 myriads of

1 In 'Treatise on the Palaces', *Zohar*, I.
2 Mohammed Qazwini, Persian scholar.
3 Al Hakem from Ibn Omar.
4 Psalms lxviii, 17.
5 Daniel vii, 10.
6 Revelation v, 11.

angels—in Greek a 'myriad' meant originally ten thousand, more loosely an innumerable quantity—others say 499,000 myriads. This would give us an angel population of around five billion. The number put forward by the Cabbalists in the fourteenth century—301,655,722—comprises, apparently, only the angels who come to earth, a tiny minority of the heavenly population. But we should consider this as only a provisional estimate and one widely exceeded today, since in Jewish thought creation is unfinished, and God can continue to make angels every day if it appeals to Him. And so they can sing: 'Every day the Most Holy creates a legion of angels who recite a canticle before him, then depart.'[1]

How do we set about doing our angelic sum? Jews play their own game of numbers and letters, with each letter in the Hebrew alphabet—there are twenty-two in all—being also a number: so the first nine letters correspond to numbers 1 to 9; the following nine to the tens—that is, from 10 to 90; and the last four count as 100, 200, 300 and 400. All that is needed, then, is to find an explicit passage.

For example, we can 'measure' God's height[2] by taking a verse from a psalm of King David[3] which contains the words, 'Great is the Lord', then adding the French Bible's statement that He is 'full of strength'. Our Lord's height, we can deduce, is equal to the numerical value of 'full of strength': in Hebrew, *verav koah*, which is 236,000 parasangs (an old Persian measurement). If we round up the parasang to five kilometres, which is roughly its value, God would then be 1,180,000 kilometres tall.

He is even taller, since commentators are quick to add that a divine parasang measures three miles, a mile being 1,760 yards and one yard being four spans (the distance between the tip of the thumb and the little finger when the hand is outstretched); and one divine span contains the whole world, since 'He measured the heavens with one span.' So it is less a question of measuring God, which is an impossible task, and more a question of preventing vertigo when we attempt

1 *Bereshit Rabbah*, 78.
2 In *Hekhalot Zutartei* (The Smaller Book of Palaces), Jewish mystical text.
3 Psalm cxlv, 3.

to get some idea of His vertiginous universe: 'his greatness is unsearchable,' King David's verse goes on to say.

For Christians, creation was over by the end of the sixth day. Therefore, the number of angels must be finite. But that's just as unimaginable. Saint Cyril of Jerusalem explains that one way of calculating the number of these beings is to start with the space they occupy. Since the Earth, says Cyril, is but a grain of dust compared to the immense bowl of the heavens that envelops us all around, and since the heavens are full of angels, it has to be acknowledged that they form an incalculable multitude—all the more so given that beyond the heavens are heavens upon heavens, which are also inhabited ... Cyril concludes that the number of angels is beyond all imagining.

Saint Hilary and Saint Ambrose found numerical enlightenment in the famous parable about the lost sheep:

> What man of you, having an hundred sheep, if he lose one of them, doth not leave the ninety and nine in the wilderness, and go after that which is lost, until he find it?
>
> And when he hath found it, he layeth it on his shoulders, rejoicing.
>
> And when he cometh home, he calleth together his friends and neighbours, saying unto them, Rejoice with me; for I have found my sheep which was lost.
>
> I say unto you, that likewise joy shall be in heaven over one sinner that repenteth, more than over ninety and nine just persons, which need no repentance.[1]

They saw the angels as the ninety-nine faithful sheep, and the human race as the lost one. The angels would therefore be ninety-nine times more numerous than humans—ninety-nine times all humans ever born—past, present and future. Not exactly an easy sum to work out ...

Christians can also calculate the number of angels by taking the number of demons, which are thought to be fallen angels, since they know that according to the Book of Revela-

1 Luke xv, 4–7.

tion these amount to a third of the angelic population.[1] Demonologists who flourished not in the Middle Ages, as is often supposed, but at the beginning of the Renaissance—a good time for burning witches—did a head count of demons. Jean Wier, physician to the Duke of Burgundy, made it 7,459,126. In the fifteenth century the Cardinal Archbishop of Tusculum found that there were 133,306,668, a number that you then double to obtain the number of holy angels: 266,613,336. In the space of one century the cardinal showed a deficit of 35,042,386 angels, if we compare his calculations with those of the Jews of the Cabbala . . . Where did they all go?

Once again, the value of numbers in the Scriptures is symbolic, and the only purpose of these supposedly scholarly calculations is to make us dizzy. Their imagined precision commands our imaginations to imagine the unimaginable.

In the Koran, angels tend to come in thousands: 'I am sending to your aid a thousand angels in their ranks';[2] 'Is it not enough that your Lord should send down three thousand angels to help you?';[3] 'God will send to you five thousand angels',[4] and so on. Which suggests that their numbers are great, but indeterminate. 'To give you an idea, there is a mosque in heaven to which, ever since the creation of the universe, seventy thousand angels have come every day to celebrate their service of prayers, never to return. That is, every day seventy thousand *new* angels come to this mosque to say their prayers.'[5] If we were able to calculate how many years there have been since the Big Bang, and multiplied that number by 365, then multiplied that by 70,000, the answer would be beyond our comprehension. All we need to know is that when a man has succeeded in reading the Koran from start to finish, sixty thousand angels, so it is said, come to pray over him. That's not bad going.

1 'And [the Dragon's] tail drew the third part of the stars of heaven, and did cast them to the earth', Revelation xii, 4. In the text, the Dragon is the devil, the stars are the angels.

2 Koran viii, 9.

3 Koran iii, 24.

4 Koran iii, 25.

5 Muhammad Hamidulla, *Les Notions islamiques sur l'ange* (Islamic Ideas about Angels).

In short, we can all agree that 'None knows the warriors of your Lord but Himself'.[1]

WHY SO MANY?

Let us leave the last word to the 'angelic doctor', Saint Thomas Aquinas: 'It must, then, be said that the multitude of angels, immaterial substances, vastly outnumber all material multitudes. This is what Dionysius said: "The blessed armies of the celestial spirits are numerous, far surpassing the feeble limits of our material numbers."[2] In fact, as divine creation has the perfection of the universe as its principal aim, the more perfect human beings have become, the more God has created them in abundance.'[3]

Through this illuminating reasoning we can understand why there are more men than there are French poodles—which is something we should be glad about!

---

1 Koran lxxiv, 31.
2 Dionysius the Areopagite, *The Celestial Hierarchy*, XIV, 1.
3 *Summa Theologiae*, Ia pars, Q.50, a3.

Chapter Three

Angels and Sex

*In which we discover that an untrue anecdote conceals a
true story; follow the unseemly adventures of the two strange
angels who desert the heavens in order to seduce women
and sow desolation upon Earth before the Flood; learn what
happens afterwards to them and to their giant children; and
begin to quiz ourselves on the question of evil.*

Titillating though this subject may be, it is not new.

It goes back to the early days of April 1453, when Sultan
Mehmed II appeared before Constantinople at the head of
an army of three hundred thousand Turks, followed by a
fleet of four hundred ships. His intentions were clearly not
friendly. The Byzantine emperor Constantine XII had only
ten thousand garrison troops at his disposal for the defence
of the city. But instead of uniting against the enemy the citizens were busy tearing each other apart in a great contro-
versy, the subject of which was far too captivating for them
to allow themselves to be distracted by reality, threatening
though it was. For while they were under siege, the Byzantine
lords were discussing angels' sex organs. And so it was that
Constantinople fell like a ripe fruit into the hands of the
Turks at one o'clock in the morning of 29 May 1453, and
that in a gesture of triumph Mehmed sent the embalmed head
of the emperor Constantine on a tour of various towns of
his new empire.

The anecdote is renowned. Everything in it is true, except,
alas! the bit for which it is famous: the people of Constantinople were certainly arguing, vehemently, with many an
oblique syllogism and theological quibble—but about an

eventual union with the pope of Rome. Notwithstanding, this 'Byzantine quarrel' has passed into modern French parlance: *discuter du sexe des anges*—discussing angels' sex organs— means 'wasting time', or as the French describe it even more graphically, 'buggering flies'.

The point is, since angels are spirits, pure spirits, what could any sexual organs be attached to? Since the Second Council of Nicaea in 787, Catholicism has taught that angels have no bodies. And the Koran states categorically that they have 'no attributes of male or female sex'.[1] However, this question of angels' sexual organs is real—not because of some loony mystic's sudden enlightenment nor because of the psychedelic hallucination of some sunburnt guru whose mushroom omelette has given him indigestion, but because of the Bible itself.

This is how chapter vi of Genesis, the first book of the Bible, begins (the scene takes place just before the Flood): 'And it came to pass, when men began to multiply on the face of the earth, and daughters were born unto them, That the sons of God saw the daughters of men that they were fair; and they took them wives of all which they chose.' Now, these 'sons of God' (*Benē Elohim* in Hebrew) are in fact the angels. In the Book of Job and in the Psalms, the Bible never uses this expression in any other sense. And the expression 'took them wives' is very clear. The consequence was not long in coming: 'There were giants in the earth in those days; and also after that, when the sons of God came in unto the daughters of men, and they bare children to them, the same became mighty men which were of old, men of renown.'[2]

In the Jerusalem Bible these giants are referred to as *Nephilim*, meaning 'those who have fallen'; according to the biblical commentators, these are—given the construction of the word—either angels that have fallen from heaven or the giant children that these same angels had with the daughters of men; in the French Bible this same word can also be found in Numbers, whereas in the English version it is translated once again as 'giants': 'And there we saw the giants, the sons

---

1 Koran xliii, 19.
2 Genesis vi, 4.

of Anak, which come of the giants.'[1] This is all the Bible has to say on the matter.

For details we must consult the Book of Enoch, an apocryphal Jewish manuscript dating from the second century BC, and the first known document on the angels' fall. This book is presented as a 'rediscovered story' of the patriarch Enoch, the seventh man created after Adam, great-grandfather of Noah and father of the famous Methuselah, who, unlike his son who died at the age of 969, never died at all, but disappeared in the flower of manhood—for a patriarch—at 365 years old: 'for God took him'.[2] The Book of Enoch tells of his encounters in the hereafter.

This apocryphal book, supposedly written by the antediluvian patriarch in person, now often referred to as 'the pseudo-Enoch', is the source of most Jewish angelology, just as Christian angelology finds its origin in a pseudo-Denys (or -Dionysius) the Areopagite, who attributes his text to a holy man who disappeared several centuries before his work was published. The true authors of these works were no rogues— they simply put their work out under the name of some indisputable authority who had gloriously departed this life, in order to give it more prestige.

Pseudo-Enoch has this to say in what is the earliest account of the fall of the angels: 'And it came to pass when the children of man had multiplied, that in those days were born unto them beautiful and comely daughters. And the angels, the children of the heaven, saw them and lusted after them, and said to one another: "Come, let us choose us wives from among the children of men and beget us children." '[3] And off they went, some two hundred of them, under the command of their leader Shemjaza. Each took one wife—let us not exaggerate—and instructed her in 'enchantments and root cuttings'—in short, in all sorts of wicked magic. Azazel taught men how to manufacture arms to kill one another, and jewellery to please the ladies, and, in addition, 'the use of antimony, and the beautifying of the eyelids, and all kinds

1 Numbers xiii, 33.
2 Genesis v, 24.
3 Book of Enoch, vi, 1–2, translated R.H. Charles (Oxford at The Clarendon Press, 1912).

of costly stones, and all colouring tinctures. The result was a great ungodliness.'[1] The Earth was so overrun with vice and crime that the angels' wives began to give birth to giants 'taller than three thousand cubits' who devoured 'all the fruit of man's labour', many animals and eventually men themselves—that is, when they were not eating each other.

'As men perished on the earth, a clamour rose to the heavens.' Then the archangels Michael, Uriel, Raphael and Gabriel looked down from above, saw the carnage, and went to plead mankind's cause with God. And God sorted it out. He sent Uriel to warn Noah of the imminent Flood and to teach him survival techniques; Raphael, to chain up Azazel in the desert; Gabriel, to banish the giants, who were fighting each other to the death; and Michael, to chain up Shemjaza along with his henchmen until Judgement Day.

The Book of Enoch synthesises different versions, passed down by word of mouth in Jewish tradition, of a story that was still current. According to Enoch it was through desire, and desire to procreate—both, by their very nature, impossible for angels to achieve—that they came down to Earth.

According to a ninth-century midrash (a rabbinical commentary),[2] it was a question of lust, pure and simple. But if desire was so suddenly aroused in the angels, it was the women who were the teasers: they were wandering around starkers. For these *Benoth-hāādam*, these daughters of man, were the daughters of Cain, the fratricide (who himself was the son of Eve and the serpent),[3] the father of a generation of evil creatures who, 'men and women alike, wandered around entirely naked, like animals'. These wicked women, the angels' wives, gave birth to six children at a time, who, from the moment they were born, stood up on their two legs and danced. When Noah came to warn the giants to put a stop to their idiocies, because God was threatening to drown the whole world in one massive flood, they just laughed: they

1 Enoch viii, 1–2.
2 *Sayings of Rabbi Eliezer.*
3 This tradition is based on a verse in Genesis (iii, 13) in which Eve says to God: 'The serpent beguiled me'—in Hebrew, *'Ishiani'*, which can also mean 'He put his seed on me.' Cain's wickedness, the murder of his good brother Abel, is explained by this diabolical parentage.

couldn't swim, but all they needed to do was to stand on a hill for their heads to be higher than the mountains. They should not have laughed, though, because to get rid of them God had the flood water heated up and the giants ended up in a court-bouillon.

In another, late, version[1] Shemjaza and Azazel want to come down to Earth to prove that angels are better than humans. God doubts it. But they insist, and keep telling Him that they will hallow His name on Earth and that, if they were in men's place, under the same conditions they would behave much better than they do—angelically, in fact. In the end God allows them to go off in human form. Shemjaza then falls in love with a woman called Ishtar. To seduce her, he tells her that he is an angel, and that God has taught him a miraculous word that will allow him to ascend to heaven instantly. Ishtar is curious and wants to know what this word is (it is God's own name). Shemjaza signals to her what it is through puzzles but without saying it, like a rebus, but Ishtar, being a bit of a twit, says it out loud and so finds herself instantly in heaven. As a reward for having died sinless, and so that she will always be remembered, God placed her among the seven stars in the Pleiades.

Shemjaza and Azazel did of course teach women about cosmetics, and men about the art of manufacturing arms. They married and produced two giant sons, Hiwa and Hiyya, who each ate a thousand camels, a thousand oxen and a thousand horses a day. When the Angel Metatron came to announce the Flood, Shemjaza was distraught: how could his giant little ones eat if the whole Earth were covered in water?

Then Hiwa and Hiyya had a dream: one of them saw a solid tree trunk from which grew four branches, the other four names written on the ground. Shemjaza interpreted the dream as follows: the four branches and the four names were the four people who would survive the Flood: Noah and his three sons, Shem, Ham and Japheth. The giants began to cry: for did their dream not signify that they would disappear for ever? To console them, the angel Shemjaza told them: 'Your

---

1 *Tseenah Ureenah*, 'Commentary on the Torah', by Jacob ben Isaac Ashkenazi of Janow.

names will not disappear from people's lips: whenever a man cuts wood, lifts heavy rocks, rows a boat or drives a chariot with horses or oxen, he will cry, 'Hiwa, Hiyya, Hiwa, Hiyya'[1]—the Hebrew equivalent of our 'Gee-up!' or 'Heave-ho!'

Shemjaza realised the extent of his transgression and repented: he hung himself upside down, between heaven and Earth, and he is still there today. As for Azazel, he has persisted in sinning, and continues to this day to seduce men by means of women's finery. He lives in the desert where he was sent on the Day of Atonement, in biblical times, a billy-goat loaded with all the sins of Israel: the famous scapegoat.

All three of these variations on the fall of the angels focus, for the first time, on explaining the origin of evil. Since God is good, He could not have created evil; yet evil exists— how? It is not so much the angels' monstrous progeny that is significant here—a logical consequence of the unnatural union of two different species—for it would be engulfed along with the rest of corrupt humanity in the flood waters, but rather all the vile abuses that these perverse angels have taught, such as the art of war to men, and to women the art of seduction through cosmetics; As Saint Cyprian in the third century so gallantly put it: 'The angels taught women to banish all truth from their faces and heads.'

If man commits evil, it is because his elder angel-brother has inspired him to do so, just as the snake whispered to Eve to take a bite from the forbidden fruit. Whence God's infinite mercy towards men, who are never totally responsible for their acts: when it comes to evil, it will always be the angels who are the first to blame.

But why did the angels fall? There are basically three possible explanations: lust, the desire to procreate, or vanity. In two out of the three, in short, it is a question of sex.

The fact remains that the early Christians, who were Jews, knew this story of the angels' fall. The proof is in the first epistle of Saint Paul, an old pupil of Rabban Gamaliel, to the Corinthians, where he explains that when the community comes together to worship women should wear a veil over

1 Ashkenazi, *Tseenah Ureenah*, 'Noah'.

their heads, as a sign of submission to their husbands—that goes without saying—but also 'because of the angels'.[1] They must not run the risk of seducing them with their long hair. This, at least, is how the great majority of the early Fathers of the Church, up until the fourth century, would interpret it. Saint Justin, in the second century, explained that the fallen angels, 'the demons, passing themselves off as gods, committed every sort of indecency and terrified mankind'. Clement of Alexandria spoke of their sensual excesses, and Tertullian in a treatise called them *'desertores Dei, amatores feminarum'*, 'deserters of God and lovers of women'.[2]

The early Fathers were quite embarrassed by the Book of Enoch, which was to be found neither among the books that make up the Hebrew Bible nor, of course, in their own. So they would have taken no account of it. Except that Saint Jude quotes it (in another context) in his epistle, and this text of Jude's is actually in the Christian Bible. Saint Jerome considered the Book of Enoch to be apocryphal, while recognising that it was not all to be discarded; 'but,' he wrote, 'great prudence must be exercised when searching for gold amidst the mire'. The Fathers therefore did just that, keeping the traditional Jewish belief in the angels' original fall and taking the Book of Enoch as its mythological version.

However, another interpretation of the original passage in Genesis, which first appeared with Julius the African in the third century, would be defended by Saint Caesarius in the sixth. The 'sons of God' who found 'the daughters of man' to their taste were not angels but the descendants of Seth, the gentle son born to Adam after the death of Abel. And the 'daughters of man' were the descendants of Cain, Adam's wicked son, the one who had killed his own brother. They were beautiful, according to the names they bear in Genesis: Ada, 'beauty'; Silla, the brunette; Noemi, 'the graceful one'. As for the giants, they existed before this time, and the Scriptures confirm it; they were the sons of Cain, the smiths, who built the Tower of Babel.

At the beginning of the fifth century Saint Augustine

1 I Corinthians xi, 10.
2 Tertullian, *De Idolatria*, IX.

declared himself in agreement with this version, and Saint Cyril of Alexandria did not hesitate to treat anyone who imagined anything else as an imbecile. Later Christians hardly ever referred to the story, Enoch fell out of fashion, and Saint Thomas Aquinas, picking up Saint Augustine's interpretation,[1] would find another apocryphal story to ruminate on.

But if you thought that the matter was now closed, you would be wrong.

The adventures of Shemjaza and Azazel do not stop here: for in the seventh century our two ne'er-do-wells would succeed in infiltrating the Koran, under another identity, where they can be found in verse 102 of the second sura:

> The devils . . . teach men witchcraft and that which was revealed to the angels Hārūt and Mārūt in Babylon . . . From these two, they learn a charm by which they can create discord between husband and wife . . . They learn, indeed, what harms them and does not profit them; yet they know full well that anyone who engaged in that traffic would have no share in the life to come.

Does this remind you of anything? The Koran says nothing further about it, but traditional tales do. This is roughly what they have to say:

The angels looked down from on high and saw that mankind was behaving pretty badly. They could not stop ranting about these lamentably sinful creatures. God listened to them and defied them to do better, placed under the same conditions, than mankind. The angels accepted the challenge and delegated two of their number, Hārūt and Mārūt, to be their representatives on Earth, charged with the mission of ridding it of serious sins: idolatry, fornication, murder and the drinking of wine. But once they got there, Hārūt and Mārūt immediately fell in love with a very beautiful woman called Zohra—who escaped them because God transformed her into the star Venus. After several libations, they were caught in the act when another woman was according them her favours; they did not hesitate to kill the witness of their

---

1 *Summa Theologiae, Ia pars, Q.51, a3.*

offence. Back on course, Hārūt and Mārūt continued to commit every sin in the book; they also taught astrology.

Meanwhile, God made known to the rest of the angels up there in heaven the deplorable behaviour of their angel-brothers, and they could not but agree with Him. Only one choice remained to Hārūt and Mārūt: where their punishment would take place—on Earth or directly in hell? They chose to stay at the scene of their crimes, and have remained ever since hanging by their feet in a well in Babylon, where they suffer unremitting torture. Their descendants are not giants but those 'heroes of former times' of whom Genesis speaks and who are, for Muslims, the legendary inhabitants of Mecca at the time when Ishmael, the queen of Sheba (Balqīs) and Alexander the Great (Dhū-l-Qarnayn) arrived there.

Parallels with the third Jewish version of events are very obvious. The differences are revealing, too: in the case of Hārūt and Mārūt, God himself puts these angels to the test and initiates it—they come down to Earth on His orders. A Muslim angel does not disobey. The Koran is quite clear on the subject: 'They never instruct any man without saying to him beforehand: "We have been sent to tempt you; do not renounce your faith.' . . . although they can harm none with what they learn except by God's leave.'[1] A Muslim angel can fall, but never revolt.

The Koranic commentaries talk of these 'two legendary angels' without attaching to them any basic importance.

We seem quite happy with them.

But we are wrong.

About 1945 Georges Dumézil, taking up an idea of P. de Lagarde's, suddenly plucked Hārūt and Mārūt from their Babylonian well and unmasked them: our two rogues were not of Jewish origin at all, but Persian. Dumézil saw Hārūt and Mārūt as usurped identities under which were hidden not Shemjaza and Azazel, but Haurvatāt (Integrity) and Ameratāt (Immortality), the Nasatya twins, two Avestan demigods who did not yet have the right to drink soma, a drink reserved for the gods, and who lived half in heaven, half on Earth.

1 Koran ii, 102.

This is how they are depicted in the *Mahābhārata*,[1] the sacred book of the Hindus.

One day, Haurvatāt and Ameratāt see the beautiful Sukanyā bathing naked in a pool, and fall in love with her. To put them off, she tells them that she is married to the ascetic, Cyavana. The handsome young twins protest that he is old and wizened. No doubt, she replies, but she loves him. But after some discussion, she admits that if they could rejuvenate her ancient husband she would reconsider her decision and choose a husband from among the three of them.

Then the handsome young twins bathe with the old husband in the pool, and when all three emerge from the water they look absolutely alike. But with her feminine intuition, Sukanyā chooses Cyavana again as her husband. Delighted with his unexpected youthfulness, Cyavana wants to offer the twins a glass of soma as a gesture of thanks. But now the goddess Indra intervenes: they have no right to drink soma! The ascetic Cyavana, who has more than one trick up his sleeve, instantly paralyses the goddess and creates 'through the power of penitence' a gigantic monster, Mada, Ecstasy. In terror, Indra capitulates: the twins can drink the liquor of the gods. The ascetic Cyavana then cuts Ecstasy into four pieces and puts one in drink, one in women, one in dice and one in the hunt.

Although this story recounts not a fall but a heavenly promotion, Dumézil notes that it has three things in common with the adventures of Hārūt and Mārūt: twin angels, a woman who escapes from them, and the revelation that drunkenness generates all major crime—injustice, lust and murder. He concludes, therefore, that the angels descended from the Nasatya twins. Everyone has been searching, ever since, for an explanation as to how a synthesis of traditional Persian elements and Jewish legend could have come about, and by what miracle this hypothetical synthesis could have reached Arabia at the beginning of the seventh century. These are the findings: it seems that these stories were in the air, that there was a great deal of mobility in the region, for whatever reason, and a lot of interaction between people,

1 *Mahābhārata*, III, 123–5.

and so inevitably the stories intermingled. Or maybe not. Like parallel lines, mythologies always give the impression of meeting on the distant horizon.

Be that as it may, Talmudic Judaism has kept the story of the fallen angels, Shemjaza and Azazel, but without attaching any more importance to it than Islam has to that of Hārūt and Mārūt. Philosophical Judaism calls them 'exotic plants with brilliant flowers, but without roots in Judaism'—in other words, they were the legends brought back by the Jews from their captivity in Babylon and later assimilated.

Christian theologians, for their part, sorted it all out in about the fifth century by assimilating the 'sons of God' with the descendants of Seth and 'the daughters of man' with those of Cain—although at the time most of them were working from texts translated into Greek or Latin, and nowhere in the Hebrew Bible are the sons of Seth called *Benē Elohim*, 'Sons of God', meaning angels.

On a popular level—for angels are, in every time and place, closer to the people than to theologians—reminders of these enigmatic and lascivious beings, to be found deep inside the four mysterious Bible verses, persist in paintings and sometimes in sculptures, on the walls, capitals and tympanums of medieval churches. Take a look at them: the good angels are draped and sexless, while the bad ones, the demons, are naked and hairy, and never miss an opportunity to show their pointed willies.

But in Christian teaching, demons are angels. Therefore they have no sex organs. Consequently the 'father of falsehood' exhibits an imaginary, dummy sex organ in order, one might say, to cock a snook at his stupid little human brothers who have the real thing. However, demons would never consent to this sort of illusionistic striptease if sex did not have an altogether special importance in regard to God Himself.

Man, God's last creation, is the only one to be made in the image of God Himself[1]—that is, he is both spiritual and creative. This creativity, which is unique to humans, is manifested not only in art and in technical skills but also, on the

1 Genesis i, 27.

63

simplest level, in procreation. 'Be fruitful, and multiply'[1] are, moreover, the first words that God said to humankind—and it was an order. Later, when He wants to make known his covenant with Abraham, He does not ask him to cut off the end of his nose or pierce his ears, but to regard as sacred the organ which, in man, would seem to be the closest to the animal kingdom when it is, in truth, a fundamental link with the kingdom of God.

Now, 'in angels there is no fertility, only beauty', says Father Marie-Dominique Philippe;[2] angels are far more beautiful and more intelligent than men, but they can neither create nor procreate. It's easy to see that this might make some of them mad with jealousy.

And none more than Lucifer, that most beautiful of all the angels in heaven, the one who bore the light and who burnt his wings on it.

1 Genesis i, 28.
2 Dominican priest, currently a professor of Philosophy and Theology.

Chapter Four

Satan

In which we recount the story of the wicked angel who seduced Eve, and the manner in which he did it; reveal how his conflict with God and his hatred of men began; and encounter djinns and demons, and some other hardly commendable creatures.

Why depict Satan first?

Because he is the first angel to be seen in the Bible, the first angel that man—and, as it happens, woman—meets, and the cause of mankind's greatest misfortunes.

The worm was in the apple right from the beginning, if we dare say it. Hardly had Adam and Eve emerged from the hands of their Creator for their joyful romp in the Garden of Eden than he was there.

It is not easy to identify him. To make his entrance, this angel, this demon, played the fool, disguised himself as a snake 'more subtil than any beast of the field which the Lord God had made'.[1] And it is not easy, either, to imagine what this snake would have looked like. The innumerable pictures, frescos and other illustrations showing him coiled round the tree of the forbidden fruit, and on one side Eve with her long hair and on the other Adam with his leaves, cannot be described as very realistic. At the time—that is, *before* God condemned him, for his sin, to go about 'upon [his] belly' and 'eat dust all the days of [his] life'—the snake had not yet become a reptile—otherwise, this divine curse would have been meaningless.

---

1 Genesis iii, 1.

When the serpent appeared to Eve he neither climbed nor coiled himself round things, but stood up, on feet. So what did he look like? According to some rabbinical commentaries of the first century, he was of the size and appearance of a camel. According to others, he had the shape of a snake but 'with feet and hands as those of a man, and wings on his shoulders, six on the right side and six on the left side'.[1]

What we do know is that our grandmother Eve found him seductive. What should have put her on her guard was when she heard the snake speak—hardly a natural thing for an animal to do. Furthermore, he spoke in a language hitherto unknown (until then, Adam and Eve had never heard anyone speak except God): he spoke the language of lies. The serpent 'said unto the woman: Yea, hath God said: Ye shall not eat of every tree of the garden?'

This very first lie is amusing. It is not the opposite of the truth, but a parasite of it. By that I mean that it is not a new remark, but one attached to an earlier one: the Word of God. God had told man that he could eat fruit from all the trees in the garden, except the tree of the knowledge of good and evil. Instead of saying to the woman, 'God has said "You must eat from no tree in the garden"'—in which case Eve would have cried out indignantly and drawn his attention to all the trees she could eat from—the serpent uttered this ambiguous question: 'So you don't eat from all the trees in the garden?', which obliged her, when she answered, to highlight the one forbidden tree as more important, to her, than all the others. Like a hermit-crab, the lie would settle into truth's empty shell—after devouring the original occupant. God is the Word, Satan the meddlesome parasite.

> And the woman said unto the serpent, We may eat of the fruit of the trees of the garden: But of the fruit of the tree which is in the midst of the garden, God hath said, Ye shall not eat of it, neither shall ye touch it, lest ye die.
>
> And the serpent said unto the woman, Ye shall not surely die: For God doth know that in the day ye eat

1 *The Apocalypse of Abraham.*

thereof, then your eyes shall be opened, and ye shall be as gods, knowing good and evil.[1]

Here also the serpent's reply is interesting; it is a beautiful lie, redolent with truth. 'Ye shall not surely die.' Adam and Eve would not, in fact, drop dead on the spot in the garden (Adam would live until he was 930), but they would become as God had told them, 'punishable by death'—that is to say, mortal. Now God had created man as immortal: 'through the envy of the devil came death into the world',[2] goes a saying attributed to King Solomon. Satan's first present to mankind was death, which demarcates the kingdom of the 'prince of this world': Satan has no power in eternity, which is God's time. Satan is here in momentary time, mankind's time, and at this moment he has the upper hand.

There was a second consequence: 'Ye shall be as gods, knowing good and evil.' Being more intelligent than man, the angel knows good and evil and offers him the power to 'play the devil' like himself—in an illusory way, 'thinking of himself as a god', in place of God Himself. God had created man beyond good and evil; Satan would present a challenge to His authority. Man would be a god for mankind; he would choose to replace God's law—which up until that moment had been limited to the one taboo—with his own innumerable laws.

The result would not be long in coming. As soon as Adam and Eve bit into the forbidden fruit, 'the eyes of them both were opened, and they knew that they were naked; and they sewed fig leaves together, and made themselves aprons. And they heard the voice of the Lord God walking in the garden in the cool of the day: and Adam and his wife hid themselves . . .'[3] Once in the grip of knowledge, these grandparents of ours had an artful look about them. Before He chased them out of their earthly paradise, God—history's first tailor—went to the trouble of making them some 'coats of skins'.[4]

1 Genesis iii, 2–5.
2 *The Wisdom of Solomon*, II, 24.
3 Genesis iii, 7–8.
4 Genesis, iii, 21.

Over the years, owing to a fifth-century error in translation, the forbidden fruit has become an apple. 'In Latin, *pomum* is a general word for "fruit", and *malum* is an apple. With *mal* also approximating the Latin word for "evil", the link between the two happened almost naturally,' Jean-Baptiste de Vilmorin explained.[1] But in fact, the fruit was a fig—which is logical, since leaves from the fig tree were the first *cache-sexe* worn by Adam and Eve, and the first leaves to be used by artists depicting them before they were supplanted by vine leaves in the early Middle Ages.

Another error, which spread curiously enough, was the imagined link between this 'forbidden fruit' and the sex organs. No doubt it was all those pictures of little leafy underpants that started it. How else can we explain the survival of those bizarre legends in medieval bestiaries? One of them maintains that the bull elephant, being the coldest of animals, cannot mate with a female elephant unless it has first eaten mandrake—hence the idea that the fruit that Eve gave Adam was this aphrodisiac mandrake. Adam ate some of it, was seized with sudden desire and knew Eve (in the biblical sense), thus engendering Cain. As Émile Mâle, an expert on such matters, so succinctly puts it, 'The most suspect elements of ancient science and the most questionable Christian exegesis come together, as one can see, in the bestiaries.'[2]

For Adam and Eve had been created, with the order to multiply themselves and all the wherewithal to do so, *before* taking the bite from the forbidden fruit. The rabbinical commentaries, moreover, vary in their opinions on this only as to the exact hour that they did it: between the seventh and ninth hours of the day they were created. They are unanimous about the act itself. Christian tradition, on the other hand, teaches that they could have done it, but didn't have the time.[3]

---

1 In *Le Jardin des hommes* (The Garden of Mankind).

2 In *L'Art religieux du XIIIe siècle en France* (Religious Art in Thirteenth-century France), I, ch. 2.

3 'If our first parents did not have sexual relations in Paradise, it is,' Saint Augustine says, 'because they were chased out of paradise for the sin shortly after woman was created.' Thomas Aquinas, *Summa Theologiae*, Ia pars Q. 98, art. 2.

But who the devil is this Satan and why does he hound men so relentlessly? The Bible offers us little information on this. The Devil can, of course, be found in the Bible under the name of Satan, but without any explanation as to his origin or past, or any clue to his general history.

First of all, then, his name: Satan, in Hebrew, means 'the adversary', translated into Greek by the neologism *diabolos*[1] ('he who throws himself between'), which gives us our Devil. But Satan is not God's adversary—he is only one of His creatures. Satan and God are not fighting in the same arena—Satan is *man's* adversary. He wishes to prove to God that He was wrong to place His confidence in a creature of an inferior nature to his own. It is very clear, of course, that the Satan of the Bible is an angel.

In the Old Testament, which allots him little space, Satan is a sort of public prosecutor: he makes his way among the angels of God, 'going to and fro in the earth, and . . . walking up and down in it',[2] and suggests to Him that he should put Job, a just man whom God justly finds quite splendid, to the test. The question is, would Job still go on praising his Creator if all his goods were taken from him and he were stricken with illness? God allows Satan to plunge Job into misfortune, on condition that he does not drive him to suicide. But Job, sick, poor as only he knows how to be, and abandoned by everyone, remains faithful. Of course he will be rewarded, but Satan will not be punished for his role in all this: he was only doing his job.

Likewise, in Zechariah, Satan stands to the right of Joshua, to accuse him. 'The Lord rebuke thee,' the angel of God says to him.[3] He is beginning to irritate everybody, while only ever acting with God's permission. When Saul falls out of favour with God and into a deep depression, it is said that 'an evil spirit *from the Lord* troubled him'.[4]

Satan would not become autonomous until the fourth century BC, in the Book of Chronicles: 'And Satan stood up against Israel, and provoked David to number [i.e., to

1 *Diabolos* divides, as opposed to *symbolos*, which unites.
2 Job ii, 2.
3 Zechariah iii, 2.
4 I Samuel xvi, 14.

slaughter] Israel'[1]—which, as a consequence, earned David
the wrath of God and Israel a fine plague. But even here, it
is not said that Satan was disobedient in any way, even if he
did seem to be taking more and more liberties.

The rabbis' Satan is to be found in the Hebrew Bible: all
in the service of God, Satan is charged as agent provocateur,
with seducing men, accusing them before God and inflicting
death upon them. Except for one day when he has no rights
at all: his annual leave is the Day of Atonement. The proof
is in the Hebrew, where, as we saw earlier, each letter has a
number: the numerical value of his name, Ha-Satan, is 364.
On the 365th day, Satan shuts up shop. QED.

Neither the Talmud nor the midrashim, the commentaries,
mention that, as well as carrying out his official role as public
pain in the neck to the human race, Satan is also chief of
all the evil spirits. There are evil spirits aplenty in the Old
Testament, and they take various forms. There are the
seraphim, or snake-demons, who fly about burning things;
the *se'irim* (hairy demons) of the satyr variety, which take
the form of cows or goats; the *siyyim*, yelping beasts of the
desert; the *'ochim*, plaintive beasts in the shape of jackals or
owls; *iyyim*, wolves; and ostriches, 'daughters of gluttony',
and so on. And that is not counting the famous she-devil
Lilith, the 'spectre of the night',[2] a winged character with
long hair who was supposedly the first wife of Adam and
about whom all sorts of terrifying legends have abounded
ever since.

The belief in demons is deeply implanted throughout Jewish literature, which often talks of *mazziqin*, *sedim* and other
malevolent spirits. While some think that these beings are
descended, as we saw in the last chapter, from the giants
born of the antediluvian union of fallen angels and women,
the Talmud believes that demons were created directly by
God, on the sixth and last day of creation, when nightfall
interrupted His work: 'These are the demons whose souls the
Holy One (blessed be He) created, but when He was on the
point of creating their bodies the holiness of the Sabbath

1 I Chronicles xxi, 1.
2 Isaiah xxxiv, 14; Psalms xci, 15.

caught up with Him and He could not create them. May this be a warning to Israel to cease work at the approach of the Sabbath.'[1] How, otherwise, can we explain how God, who is perfect, could have created beings so far from perfect—in fact, downright unpleasant?

These half-finished demons, whether visible or invisible, fall midway between man and angel: 'Demons resemble angels in three ways; in three others they resemble men. Like angels, they have wings, they can move from one distant part of the earth to another, and they can foresee the future. Like men, they eat and drink, procreate and die.'[2] Demons are everywhere, though they have a preference for the desert, tombs and ruins. They have sex organs—whence the adventures of incubi and succubi fornicating with humans; the *Zohar* (*The Book of Splendour*), a fundamental cabbalistic text, tells us that Lilith, the queen of the demons, excites men deprived of women in order to make bodies from the sperm they release. So every man will have some demon children floating around in the air,[3] the fruit of his erotic dreams and his masturbation.

A third tradition maintains that these demons are fallen men, descendants of those who built the Tower of Babel, and that they were transformed into monkeys or demons as a punishment for their pride.[4] Jewish thought is not dogmatic, but kaleidoscopic: it thrives on contradictions, questions, new developments. Nothing is ever cut and dried—quite the opposite, in fact, for if it were, it would mean death to the Book.

Since Satan was an angel, he could not be disobedient. Stuffed with evil ideas with regard to mankind, it was only with God's permission that he could put them into practice. In the Talmud, demons are quite gentle; only on certain occasions will they harm mankind, and they soon cool down when a rabbi has a word with them. However, there is a late Jewish tradition, in one of the first-century Apocrypha, *The Life of Adam and Eve*, which makes Satan a disobedient

---

1 Judah the Prince, known as 'Rabbi'.
2 *Hagigah*, 16a; *Avot of Rabbi Nathan*, ch. 37.
3 Gershom G. Scholem, *The Cabbala and its Symbolism*, IV, 6.
4 *Sanhedrin*, 109a.

angel. In this book the angel Michael asks the other angels to follow his example in bowing before the newly created Adam. But Satan refuses, saying that Adam is not so old as he is, and of inferior rank as far as creatures go. Furious, God banishes him, and along with him all his angel dependants.

Though this last tradition has scarcely gained widespread acceptance in Jewish thought, there is a trace of it, synthesised in a single sentence, in Saint Paul's Epistle to the Hebrews: 'When he bringeth in the firstbegotten into the world, he saith, And let all the angels of God worship him.'[1] But there is nothing, afterwards, to say what Satan did.

In fact, the Koran is the only one of the official sacred scriptures to say what happened to Satan before the Garden of Eden. In the Koran he has the name of Iblīs, and the story of his fall is taken up in four suras.[2] This is what the thirty-eighth has to say:

Your lord said to the angels: 'I am creating man from clay. When I have fashioned him and breathed My spirit into him, kneel down and prostrate yourselves before him.'

The angels all prostrated themselves except Satan, who was too proud, for he was an unbeliever.

'Satan,' said He, 'why do you not bow to him whom My own hands have made? Are you too proud, or do you deem yourself superior?'

Satan replied: 'I am nobler than he. You created me from fire, but him from clay.'

'Begone, you are accursed!' said He. 'My curse shall remain on you until the Day of Reckoning.'

He replied: 'Reprieve me, Lord, till the Day of Resurrection.'

He said: 'Reprieved you shall be till the Appointed Day.'

'I swear by Your glory,' said Satan, 'that I will seduce them all except your faithful servants.'[3]

1 Hebrews i, 6.
2 Suras vii, xv, xx and xxxviii.
3 Koran xxxviii, 71–83.

And he begins with Adam and Eve in their earthly paradise. In another sura[1] Iblīs spells out to God his programme for mankind: 'I shall . . . spring upon them from the front and from the rear, from their right and from their left. Then You will find the greater part of them ungrateful.'

So Satan disobeyed God by refusing to prostrate himself before man, a creature who appeared inferior to him; but, though cursed, he received authorisation from God to pester mankind. His power is restricted, he can do nothing against true believers, who, what is more, have been well and truly put on their guard. 'Do not walk in Satan's footsteps; he is your inveterate foe'[2] is nothing less than a constant refrain throughout the Koran. Under divine control, as he is in the Bible, Satan tries to prove to God that man is a creature unworthy of His confidence.

In Islam, it is not at all certain whether Satan is an angel, precisely because angels are impeccable and cannot disobey God. Now Iblīs, by not prostrating himself before Adam, disobeyed. So he is not an angel. But if he is not an angel, God's command, which was addressed to the angels, was of no concern to him, so he could not have disobeyed.

Tradition has generally opted for regarding Iblīs as a djinn. Heirs of the biblical demons and comparable to the Greek *daimon* while at the same time typically Islamic, djinns are creatures intermediate between men and angels. The angels are made of light, djinns of fire, and men of earth. A djinn can be good, such as the one who inhabited Aladdin's lamp, or bad, in which case he is called *shaytān*, or demon. Djinns are invisible, but they can take on various shapes and enter into the bodies of different animals: cats, birds, snakes, scorpions, horses, camels . . . 'Their true form is similar to humans', but their bellies are like bones, with no cavity and no intestines. They eat only if they want to, sleep very little and produce no excrement.'[3] Gifted with the power of reason, djinns have sex organs, reproduce, and die.

And there is another argument for making Iblīs a djinn:

---

1 Koran vii, 17.
2 Koran: e.g., II, 208; xii, 5; xvii, 53; xxxv, 6.
3 Mohammad Mokri.

he has children, which he engenders at the insistence of his wife, Anger—but all on his own. 'Iblīs has both sex organs: the male on his right leg, the female on his left. He fertilises himself and lays ten eggs a day. From each egg emerge seventy *shaytān* and *shaytāna*. The *shayātīn* are both male and female. Like all djinns they reproduce more rapidly than other creatures, since they are of a fiery nature.'[1]

According to legend, before the creation of Adam, Satan-Iblīs was called Azāzīl. He was a very handsome and very pious djinn. With God's permission, the angels led him up to the heavens where he became their leader and instructor. He lived in heaven at night and on Earth during the day, where he was given the task of guiding the djinns along the right path. But his privileged position eventually went to his head, and he refused to bow before Adam.

If Satan is the father of a multitude of *shayātīn* he certainly cannot, for Muslims, be the leader of legions of revolting angels—this is a typically Christian idea, but one that will be elaborated over the centuries.

At the time when the Koran was written, Christianity had already abandoned the idea of demons as sons of men and angels. Origen, in the third century, was the first to banish the stories of Enoch to the apocryphal dustbins. From the fourth century onwards, under his influence, the Greek and then the Latin Church ceased to see demons as half-angelic, half-human beings, but rather as angels subordinate to Satan, who fell at the same time as he did. He found a source for them in Saint John's Apocalypse (the Book of Revelation):

And there was war in heaven: Michael and his angels fought against the dragon; and the dragon fought and his angels,

And prevailed not; neither was their place found any more in heaven.

And the great dragon was cast out, that old serpent, called the Devil, and Satan, which deceiveth the whole

---

1 Toufic Fahd, 'L'islam et ses sectes' (Islam and its Sects), in *Histoire des religions* (History of Religions), III, La Pléiade, Gallimard.

world: he was cast out into the earth, and his angels were cast out with him.[1]

The text gives not the number of these fallen angels, but a proportion. In fact, the tail of the Dragon swept 'the third part of the stars of heaven, and did cast them to the earth'.[2] From this it can be concluded that a third of the angels fell. Although the Apocalypse was supposedly talking about the end of the world and not its beginning, this explanation spread to the exclusion of all others.

Until Origen, the cause of Satan's sin was, more or less, what the Koran describes: Satan was jealous of Adam, of man. When God made Adam master of the Earth, Satan was furious to see himself stripped of his privileges and laid a trap in the Garden of Eden; and so it was that by dragging Adam into sin Satan also sinned. It was clear to everybody, even if neither the masses nor the theologians were much moved by it, that Satan's sin was jealousy.

Origen would put the boot into this theory, well and truly. For in his view, the devil had already fallen into evil ways *before* the creation of Adam: 'He was a murderer from the beginning,' Jesus said,[3] and so the explanation of his fall should be sought elsewhere than in the jealousy he felt for mankind, who had not yet been created. Origen found it in the prophet Isaiah's description of the death of the king of Babylon. There is no doubt that it was the Devil that was at issue, and that these words were addressed to him:

How art thou fallen from heaven, O Lucifer, son of the morning! how art thou cut down to the ground, which didst weaken the nations!

For thou has said in thine heart, I will ascend into heaven, I will exalt my throne above the stars of God: I will sit also upon the mount of the congregation, in the sides of the north:

1 Revelation xii, 7–9.
2 Revelation xii, 4.
3 John viii, 44.

I will ascend above the heights of the clouds; I will be like the most High'.[1]

The angel called 'the morning star', otherwise known as Lucifer, 'he who bears the light', was led astray through pride. Ezekiel adds:

Thou art the anointed cherub that covereth; and I have set thee so: thou wast upon the holy mountain of God; thou hast walked up and down in the midst of the stones of fire.

Thou wast perfect in thy ways from the day that thou wast created, till iniquity was found in thee.

By the multitude of thy merchandise they have filled the midst of thee with violence, and thou hast sinned: therefore I will cast thee as profane out of the mountain of God: and I will destroy thee, O covering cherub, from the midst of the stones of fire.

Thine heart was lifted up because of thy beauty, thou hast corrupted thy wisdom by reason of thy brightness; I will cast thee to the ground, I will lay thee before kings, that they may behold thee.'[2]

Similis ero Altissimo: 'I shall be like unto High and Mighty God'—such was Satan's transgression. A spiritual nature cannot sin against the flesh, only against the spirit. Now, jealousy is a sin against the flesh; but pride, subsequently listed as number one in the top ten of mortal sins, is not. Hypotheses vary as to where this diabolical pride came from. For Satan, a first-class seraph, is far from stupid—he is, in fact, sublimely intelligent.

Rupert de Deutz, Benedictine abbot of Tuy in the twelfth century, explained that Lucifer, being blind to the truth of the matter, boasted to the other angels that he was self-generated. There was nothing the angels could say to this by way of contradiction: since Lucifer had been created the first,

1 Isaiah xiv, 12–14.
2 Ezekiel xxviii, 14–17.

his creation had had no other witness but God Himself. So Satan would have liked to pass himself off as God amongst his peers. For Saint Thomas Aquinas, Satan would have liked to owe his happiness to none other than himself, and would in so doing equate himself to God. But Father Francesco Suarez, a sixteenth-century Spanish Jesuit theologian, found Saint Thomas's thesis unworthy of the great spirit that is Lucifer, and offered another. He thought that from the beginning God had made known to the angels his project of uniting, in Jesus, the Word with a man, and that Satan had been furious to see this privilege accorded to a creature of the human race instead of to the most perfect of creatures, an angel—and to the most perfect of angels, himself.

The debate is far from over, except for the basic premise: that Satan wished to be God's equal. This corroborates not only what he said to Eve, 'Ye shall be as the gods', but also the manner in which he behaved towards Jesus in the Gospels. Jesus had fasted for forty days in the desert when he met Satan, who put him to the test three times. The last of these temptations is like a parody of the scene later described in the Koran:

Again, the devil taketh him up into an exceeding high mountain, and sheweth him all the kingdoms of the world, and the glory of them;

And saith unto him, All these things will I give thee, if thou wilt fall down and worship me.

Then saith Jesus unto him, Get thee hence, Satan: for it is written, Thou shalt worship the Lord thy God, and him only shalt thou serve.[1]

Here it is very clear that Satan is posturing as God's rival on Earth. Jesus, who calls him 'prince of this world', sends him packing to the farthest reaches of his principality: material goods, power and glory may well be his, but only down below. Jesus, exorcising a mass of demons, repeats that his kingdom 'is not of this world'.

1 Matthew iv, 8–10.

Satan, as we have seen, is the enemy of man. The existence of Jesus, simultaneously man and God, definitely unhinges him: the formerly polite prosecutor of mankind is furious. Jesus is not going to conquer him with a display of divine omnipotence, though, but rather through his humility and by abandoning himself to his all too human frailty. He is going to die—that is, undergo the punishment that Satan himself has brought upon mankind—so that man, through him, will be saved for all time: 'through death he might destroy him that had the power of death, that is, the devil,' wrote Saint Paul.[1] Through his death, an apparent defeat, Jesus has conquered death. Satan himself will never die,[2] and he knows that he is already lost—which does nothing to calm him down.

It is Jesus' dual nature, human and divine, that rouses Satan's anger; the latter's presence is therefore much more invasive in Christianity than anywhere else. He can display himself even better there, since Christians, unlike Jews and Muslims for whom figurative representation is prohibited, are not going to stint themselves as regards either paintings or carvings of the enemy and his henchmen. At Vézelay in Burgundy, for example, the hairy devils had a distinctly punk look as early as the twelfth century.

All Christian theologians make Satan a fallen angel—'an extracelestial entity who squats in the world for a brief spell', according to Chesterton, and the first of all the angels. But if Satan and his hellhounds are pure spirits, invisible, this in no way inhibits them from appearing in the guise of horrible beasts, humans or even angels, to torment Christians—preferably saints. Father Claude Nicolas, exorcist at Notre-Dame de Paris, explains this well: 'Most people behave so badly that the devil has no reason to show himself to them overtly: he is already acting in their hearts. It tends to be mystics who are the object of demoniacal vexations.'[3]

There are countless examples, from Saint Paul—'there was

---

1 Hebrews ii, 14.
2 He will burn in the eternal fire along with his angels and the damned: cf. Matthew xxv, 41.
3 In *Le Démon de l'angoisse* (The Demon of Anxiety), Bayard, Centurion.

given to me a thorn in the flesh, the messenger of Satan to buffet me'[1]—to the Curate of Ars, and including the famous temptations of Saint Antony, and Saint Martin who saw the devil trying to take the form of Christ himself. In the thirteenth century, a German Cistercian monk explained in a work intended for novices that demons could even contaminate food: that a demon could hide in a glass of milk – swallow it and you die![2] At the beginning of the fifteenth century, Saint Frances of Rome was so infuriated by Satan dragging her by the hair that she had it cut off so as to take the veil. In the nineteenth century, every night for more than thirty years the Curate of Ars received stormy visits from someone whom he nicknamed 'The Grab'.[3] This visitor tossed the curtains about, scraped the floor and shook the walls of his room—when he wasn't setting fire to it. 'Since he was unable to have the bird, he wanted to burn its cage,' the saintly priest commented unemotionally. 'We have had dealings with each other for a while now, and we have got to know one another—we are companions ... The demon is quite shrewd, but he has no staying power: a sign of the cross puts him to flight.'

These demoniacal visitations, to be frank, are not reserved for Catholics alone: Martin Luther saw the devil in monkeys and parrots, animals that can cleverly mimic man or his voice. He tells how in 1521, when he was in hiding at the castle of Wartburg after his break with Rome, he had a battle with Satan who bombarded him with nuts from the stove in his room. Luther adds that he defended himself, from his bed, by throwing an inkwell in his face.

That was not invented.

As for Mephistophelian tales of pacts with the devil, which have flourished in literature, theatre and opera, they all derive from the *Miracle of Theophilus*, which was a phenomenal success in medieval times. The action takes place in 537, in the East. Theophilus, vidame[4] of the Bishop of Adana in

---

1 II Corinthians xii, 7.
2 Caesarius d'Heisterbach, *Dialogus miraculorum*.
3 In the French, *'le Grappin'*—a *grappin* was a sort of pickaxe with three claws, used at the time on farms'.
4 Assistant and representative in lay matters.

Cilicia, is so virtuous that when his bishop dies the people want to elect him as his successor; but Theophilus, ever modest, refuses so that he can stay on as vidame to the new bishop. Satan, however, pesters him and tempts him and infiltrates his mind with a desire for the power that he has just turned down—to the extent that Theophilus goes to see a magician and agrees to give up his soul to hell if Satan will agree, in exchange, to make him famous in this world. The pact is drawn up on a parchment. Theophilus signs. Satan appears and carries off the document.

From this moment on, Theophilus receives honours and rewards, is successful in everything he does. However, tortured by the memory of his crime, he is beset with remorse. One night, after he has been praying to the Virgin Mary, he falls asleep in the church. There he dreams that Mary appears to him, pardons his sin and gives him back the parchment that she has wrested from the devil. And when he awakes, Theophilus finds that the parchment is there in his hand. Mad with joy, he goes to the bishop to confess his sin, tells everyone the story of his crime and of his pardon, then dies in a state of holiness a few days later.[1]

This tale was translated into Greek by a Neapolitan deacon, then put into verse by a bishop, analysed in *Les Miracles de Notre-Dame* by Gautier de Coincy, sung in the eleventh-century liturgy for the Virgin Mary, transformed into a mystery play by Rutebeuf[2] in the thirteenth century, included in *The Golden Legend* by Jacob of Voragine,[3] sculpted on the north portal of Notre-Dame de Paris and on the west portal of Lyons Cathedral, and depicted in the stained-glass windows at Le Mans, Chartres, Laon, Beauvais and Troyes . . . in short, used by all the media of the time.

Today, if Satan is not part of the profession of faith, the Catholic Creed, he does appear in the Paternoster, the Lord's Prayer, the prayer of every Christian, in the last sentence:

---

1 Recounted in Émile Mâle, *L'Art religieux du XIIIe siècle en France.*

2 Rutebeuf, *c.*1249–*c.*1277, one of the most important French poets of the early Middle Ages.

3 A manual of the lives of the saints and of episodes in the lives of Jesus and Mary. Jacob of Voragine was Bishop of Genoa in the thirteenth century.

Et ne nos inducas in tentationem, sed libera nos a Malo—
translated, astonishingly, as 'And lead us not into temptation,
but deliver us from Evil' when it should say, 'And lead us
not into temptation, but deliver us from the Evil One', since
the catechism itself[1] says: 'In this request, Evil is not an
abstraction, but indicates a person, Satan, the Evil One, the
angel who opposes God.' 'Evil' gives a more presentable,
more discreet and more rational tone than 'the Evil One',
that hairy old devil of which the Dantesque description—
gigantic, three-headed, with two great 'featherless wings like
a bat's', who 'weeps with six eyes on to his three chins, from
which tears and bloody slobber drip'[2]—finally disappeared
from churches after the Council of Trent issued its directives
on good taste in 1563.

At its last council, Vatican II, the Catholic Church, which
at times appears more anxious to discard obscurantism than
the Devil, threw out many angels, good and bad, from its
liturgy. Some theologians may even have been tempted, it
seems, to consign them to the realms of mythology. In reality,
thank God, the Church in France still keeps an exorcist in
each diocese, who is never out of work and is available for
consultation not just by Catholics: if the cap fits, wear it—
for eternity.

The squaring of the satanic circle is the same for all three
monotheisms; since God is simultaneously infinitely good and
forgiving but also all-powerful, these are the questions that
have to be answered: Why is there so much hatred? Where
does evil come from?

For Jews, Satan is an angel whose mission, according to
the ancient sages of the Mishnah, is this: 'He descends to
earth and seduces, then he ascends and accuses, and finally,
having obtained permission, he takes away life.' For Muslims,
Satan is a djinn, Iblīs, who refuses to accept that God should
take a creature who is not the acme of his creation for its
centrepiece; for the angel is superior to man in both intelligence and beauty, yet it is man whom God has chosen as his
representative on Earth. Driven out of the heavens, Iblīs has

1 *Catechism of the Catholic Church*, para. 2851, Plon, 1992.
2 Dante, *The Divine Comedy*, 'Hell', Canto xxxiv.

the right to harass mankind until Judgement Day. For Christians Satan is an angel, Lucifer, who revolted against the divine plan. Created good, he became evil of his own volition and now drags all men on this Earth—whither he was expelled with his legions of angels—towards evil and death. His homicidal fury has become all the more intense since God, in Jesus Christ, became man. Every individual who succumbs to evil is in his clutches.

In any event, Satan is a sublimely intelligent being who takes God for a fool. But God is not a goof—He is good. This is His divine folly. He has chosen to focus His work neither on beauty nor on intelligence, both angelic qualities, but on goodness. When He created the world, it is not mentioned anywhere that He found it beautiful or intelligent—there is simply this refrain: 'And God saw that it was good.' Goodness is all Him; He would like men to be good 'in his image and likeness', as He had made them before this great Evil One came and suggested to them that they would be pretty stupid to go along with such a scheme.

The Devil's trick is to pass off goodness for stupidity in the eyes of man. And it is not difficult: if there is one thing that man, who is half stupid by nature anyway, cannot stand, it is to be taken for a good chap.

According to Baudelaire, 'the Devil's best trick is to persuade us that he does not exist'. In the twentieth century it was the writer André Malraux who unmasked him first: 'With the [concentration] camps Satan reappeared, visibly, in the world.'[1] How can his terrible signature *not* be seen, under Nazism? Here was a people who, dazzled by their own alleged beauty, proclaimed themselves to be the 'Aryan race' and decided to remake the world in their own dolichocephalic image—by first eliminating God's chosen people, who had become, *because* they were God's chosen people, the most troublesome witness of their crime. Some have even drawn attention to the fact that the Nazis surrendered on 8 May 1945, the feast day of St Michael, the angel who drove Satan out of heaven.

1 In *Le Miroir des limbes* (The Mirror of Limbo), part 1: *Antimémoires*, Folio, Gallimard.

Satan may be the first angel to figure in the Bible, but as my friend the gentle Brother Matthew remarks, 'He is not my favourite angel.'

Chapter Five

Angels and Their Jobs

In which we sit back and reflect on the variety of angelic messengers sent down to Earth: spies, soldiers and cavalrymen, artillerymen and police, bodyguards, firemen, lion-tamers, musicians and restaurateurs, waiters, go-betweens, undertakers and astrophysicists (angels don't know the meaning of unemployment); and in which we surprise those who are naïve enough to think that angels are useless.

What are angels for? When you think about it, perhaps we should be asking what angels are not for.

In fact, angels—the name means 'messenger'—are not defined by the sort of creature they are, but by their role. A pro to his wingtips, an angel will reveal scarcely anything of his personality except the despatch with which he carries out his role of heavenly functionary. Angels do not all, however, work at the same trade—in fact, quite the opposite: 'This is our teaching: a single angel does not fulfil two missions, and two angels do not fulfil the same mission.'[1] And the variety of their duties, at least when they come to Earth, is enormous. Quite simply, were they not here, the world would stop going round.

Angels, it seems, know nothing of trade unions: they work day and night, without time off for sleep, and far from sticking to a thirty-five-hour week they do not even have weekends off: 'The inferior orders of angels do not observe the Sabbath, so as not to bring life on Earth to a halt.'[2]

The upper orders, who form by far the greatest majority

1 *Bereshit Rabbah*, 50.
2 *Book of Jubilees*, 2.

84

of angels, never descend from the court of heaven—except for Michael, Gabriel and Raphael. Beyond a few rare high-flying mystics whose souls are sufficiently exalted to merit elevation to these lofty realms, common mortals only ever come face to face with the proletarian minority of angels.

Here follows a small—certainly not exhaustive—selection of the varied work they perform among us.

CIA: CELESTIAL INTELLIGENCE AGENCY

The image angels offer, in their perilous role of secret agent, is one of perfection; most of the time they operate quite invisibly, which just goes to show.

Should their mission demand it, they adopt a human 'cover'. The most engaging of these must be the angel Raphael in the Book of Tobit. He accomplishes his mission under a false identity that he announces without batting an eyelid: 'I am Azarias, son of Anamias the great,' he says to old Tobit, who is blind, certainly, but not deaf.

Taken on by the old man for a drachma a day, he accompanies his young son on a journey to recover his fortune, finds a fiancée for him, chases off the demon Asmodeus, and after their wedding, when he returns, finally restores the old man's sight. When old Tobit, overwhelmed with gratitude, wants to give him more money than originally planned, Raphael says: 'Surely I will keep close nothing from you. For I said, It was good to keep close the secrets of the king, but that it was honourable to reveal the works of God . . . I am Raphael, one of the seven angels which present the prayers of the saints, and which go in and out before the glory of the Holy One.'[1] Of course, the whole family practically faints with fright, but the angel reassures them—and repeats, as is the habit of angels—that it is not him they should be thanking but God. And he adds that he was only pretending to eat with them, thus revealing one of the tricks of the divine secret agent, suspected ever since the phony picnic Abraham had with the three angels in the Plains of Mamre.

Usually an angel will not reveal his true name when he

1 Book of Tobit, xii, 11, 15.

is on a visit to Earth, or only does so once his mission is accomplished, just before he leaves. This is for three reasons, at least.

First, if he says that he is an angel, it never goes down well: people tremble with fear, faint, or collapse on all fours. It can be as traumatic as it is embarrassing. This is the origin of the classic phrase, the first in the angel–man phrase book: 'Fear not!' An angel has to repeat this at least twice before the earthling can recover his composure. The second reason is that an angel has a mission to fulfil in God's name—on His behalf and in His cause. His aim is to glorify God thereby, not himself. There is no trace of vanity or pride in an angel, totally devoted to his boss as he is. His boss is without equal, the angel without ego. On the other hand, and this is the third reason, man is quick to idolise and to resort to magic; if an angel were to tell him his name he would be tempted to 'turn' him, to make him a double agent, by means of amulets and all sorts of practical booklets such as are on sale nowadays.

And none of this is new, of course. In medieval Judaism, the *Book of Raziel*—which claims to be a revelation of the angel Raziel to Adam, passed from father to son via Abraham and Moses—gives instructions on how to invoke angels according to the month, day and hour in order to obtain whatever is wanted. You would think, like the ancient Egyptian idolaters did, that no angel can resist the invocation of his name, provided it happens in the right place and at the right time: all of which leaves rather a bad smell.

False identity papers

Note that there is no need to be familiar with the real names of the angels—who could know them, anyway?—to reduce them to submission. You can just invent them. Since 'angels have the names of their offices',[1] fabricating angels turns out to be fairly easy. To do it, just take the only three angels' names given in the Bible, Michael, Gabriel and Raphael, and see how they are constructed:

1 *The Book of Raziel*, 21b.

In Hebrew, all you have to do is add the suffix *el* to the name of a thing or a function, to give it an angelic dimension. Strength, for example, is *guevura*. By adding *el* we get the angel Gavriel, or Gabriel, the messenger of strength. Healing is *rephua*; by adding *el*, the angel Raphael appears to us, and so on. Working from this, anything can become an angel if it has the divine particle *el*, signifying God, added to it. And so we get Ruhiel, angel of the wind (*ruah*), Shalgiel, the angel responsible for snow (*sheleg*), and Matariel and Kokhaviel, for rain and stars.[1]

In 1893, a painstaking scholar called Moses Schwab compiled an index 426 pages long containing the names, actual or alleged, of the angels that he had found in Hebrew manuscripts in the Bibliothèque Nationale where he worked. In it we find, for example, that if Auhabiel, 'beloved of God', is in charge of love, Pumel, 'mouth of God', has the task of beating the condemned in the sixth region of hell. Qeccefel is the angel of anger, Ishdrael of food, and Samariel is a 'divine trembling'. When a woman is suffering labour pains you must whisper in her left ear, 'Elaruss', the name of the angel of betrothals; and if you lose your memory, write the name of Aunsiel, the angel of constraint, on a wheaten cake and eat it. Anfiel, 'the face of God', will preserve you from storms. To protect yourself against wild beasts, invoke Aftiel, the angel of dusk, or Bahaliel, angel of terror, who serves the same purpose. Dahariel is 'God's gallop'. Zediel, a malicious angel, and Hazirel, 'God's pig', symbol of all things foul, have bad reputations. But Tubiel, the angel-gazelle, is invoked to catch small birds.

These inscriptions were found on clay pots, on spoons and on ancient bed legs. Serious people did not think much of them. Referring to 'the virgin forests of medieval mysticism', rabbis recalled that 'there is no enchantment against Jacob, neither is there any divination against Israel'[2]—or, at least,

---

1 Marc-Alain Ouaknin, 'Dans le double silence du nom' (In the Double Silence of the Name), in *Le Réveil des anges* (The Angels' Awakening), Autrement, Collection Mutations no. 162.
2 Numbers xxiii, 23.

there should not be. For as Rabbi Yomtov Lippman Mul-
hausen said at the end of the fourteenth century, 'Any intermediary between man and his Creator will lead to devilry
and idolatry.'

Christians, who are also much given to this type of crazy
angelical mystical-intellectual inflation, have also been made
to pull up their socks by the authorities. At the Council of
Rome in 745, the Church, under Pope Zacharias, recognised
only the names of the three angels expressly named in the
Bible: Michael, Raphael and Gabriel; all the others were
therefore to be classified, *ipso facto* and without more ado, as
belonging in the devil's camp. Under the Carolingian Empire,
after the Council of Aix-la-Chapelle in 789, anyone who
invoked any angels other than these three was excommuni-
cated forthwith. This was a terrible blow, careerwise, for the
great Uriel, 'Light of God', a name originating in the Jewish
apocrypha and by which many Christians invoked the fourth
of the seven archangels. They had also begun to build pretty
little colourwashed chapels to him.

A terrible blow, but not a fatal one, for Uriel had not yet
made his last appearance. After he had been sidelined for
seven hundred years, totally forgotten by Christians, in 1516
a fresco was revealed under the whitewash in a church in
Palermo, depicting the seven archangels, one of whom was
Uriel, duly named and 'bearing a naked sword while fire
flamed before his feet'.[1] This discovery was seen as a miracle
in Sicily; a priest, providentially named Angelo del Duca,
went off to Rome to preach this 'new' form of devotion to
the seven archangels, which met with great success as far
away as Germany and even Russia. However, Rome did not
take long to get a grip on itself, once again effacing the name
of Uriel who, it seems, has not been reinstated since, at least
with the Christians.

We must respect the heroic anonymity of God's messengers. The least we can hope of believers is that they do not
blow the cover of the Celestial Bureau's agents.

1 Émile Mâle, in *L'Art religieux du XVIIe siècle* (Religious Art of the Seventeenth
Century), Armand Colin.

Listening service

Angels put microphones even in our thoughts. 'Curse not the king, no not in thy thought; and curse not the rich in thy bedchamber: for a bird of the air shall carry the voice, and that which hath wings shall tell the matter,' says the Book of Ecclesiastes.[1] Rabbi Brown explains: 'When a man sleeps, his body talks to his mind, his mind to his soul, his soul to an angel, the angel to a cherub, the cherub to him who has wings (a seraph); and the seraph relates it all in the presence of Him whose words created the world.' This angelic relay transmission between sleeping man and God explains why man can wake feeling sad and in a bad temper without any apparent reason: it is because his soul is impure.[2]

With Muslims too, angels follow one another in succession so as to establish a permanent liaison between man and heaven. They are twenty to a man: ten during the day, relieved by ten others at night. They are called *al-Mu'aqqibāt* (blessings), for they bring down blessings from heaven at dawn prayers time, then go back to heaven in the evening, taking their good deeds with them while the bad ones remain below.

FBI: FEATHERED BODYGUARDS INCORPORATED

Escort service

'He shall give his angels charge over thee, to keep thee in all thy ways,' says the psalm numbered xci and more graciously entitled 'Under His divine wings'. 'He' is God. 'Thee' is the man who seeks refuge in God. 'They shall bear thee up in their hands, lest thou dash thy foot against a stone. Thou shalt tread upon the lion and adder: the young lion and the dragon shalt thou trample under feet.'[3]

A thousand angels make up the retinue of each son of Israel—provided he prays. And if he studies, even more. And

---

1 Ecclesiastes x, 20.
2 Jacob ben Isaac Ashkenazi of Janow, *Tseenah Ureenah*.
3 Psalms xci, 11–13.

if he does both, God himself will come to protect him. In Judaism, getting angelic assistance depends on circumstances. For example, if 999 angels pronounce a man guilty and only one says that he is innocent, God will decide in the man's favour. 'Each has guardian angels before him and behind him, who watch him by God's command', the Koran says.[1] The Prophet Mohammed explained it very prettily: 'God entrusts the believer to the care of 160 angels who hover around him invisibly: seven (in particular) hover over him like flies around a dish of honey on a summer's day.'[2]

Minders

Alongside these anonymous angels are the *Al-Hafaza*, or guardians. There are two of them: one stands on man's left and the other on his right and they record his deeds, both good and bad: once again, in Islam it is all written down. But these 'honourable scribes who know what you do'[3] are shown to be so understanding that they seem downright biased:

> The angel on the right gives his orders to his companion on the left. When a man does a good deed, he records ten good deeds. If he does a bad deed, and the left-hand companion wishes to record it, the right-hand companion says, 'Stop!' He is given six hours during which, if he asks for God's pardon, nothing will be put down on his record; if he does not, just one bad deed will be recorded.[4]

This honourable secretary goes even further: if, after six hours of reflection, he ends up writing down a bad deed and then the man does a good one, negotiations take place between him and the angel on his right with the aim of dropping a deed from somewhere on each of the lists. Allah's angels are very merciful!

1 Koran xiii, 11.
2 Qazwini, 62.
3 Koran lxxxii, 11–12.
4 Al Baihaki from Abi Ouamana.

And their good deeds live on after the man has died.

They say: 'Lord, you have caused your servant so-and-so to die. Where shall we go?'
     God replies: 'My heaven is filled with my angels who adore me and my Earth is filled with my creatures who obey me; go to the tomb of my servant, praise me, glorify me and inscribe your praises alongside the good deeds of my servant, until the day of Resurrection.'[1]

In return, when a Muslim has finished his prayer and is sitting back on his heels, knees on the ground, hands spread on his thighs (*qu'ūd*), after prostrating himself for the second time (*sujūd*) he turns his head to the right, then to the left, saying twice: 'May peace be with you and the mercy and blessings of Allah!', bowing to each side to greet each of his guardian angels. After all, it is the least he can do for these fantastic champions of his cause.
     According to the *Zohar*, Jews also benefit from the support of an angel of mercy and an angel of judgement, who record the deeds of 'the body into which He has made them enter'. Maimonides[2] understands them as good and evil tendencies.
     In the Christian tradition, the idea of having a personal good angel and a personal bad one is very widespread: 'A bad one to try us, a good one to guard us,' *The Golden Legend* says. But while this may be a popular opinion, it is not at all a Catholic one. Certainly, of the early Fathers, Hermas, Gregory of Nyssa, Origen and Cassian maintained that, as well as a good angel, everyone has a bad one: a demon. But they were the only ones to take this line. A crushing majority of theologians declared hell to be far too disorganised for this to be at all likely. The mystics, assailed by changing multitudes of devils, sided with them.

---

1 Qazwini, 60.
2 Jewish philosopher (1135–1204), author of the *Misneh Torah*, a codification of the Law, and of *The Guide of the Perplexed*, a commentary on the scriptures.

Bodyguards . . . and such close ones

So the personal guardian angel is of Christian origin. His existence is revealed in one of Jesus' admonitions regarding small children: 'Take heed that ye despise not one of these little ones; for I say unto you, That in heaven their angels do always behold the face of my Father which is in heaven.'[1] Later, but very much later, Pope Pius XII would exclaim, quite logically: 'There's no question, when children become adults, of their guardian angels abandoning them. Certainly not!' From the fifth century onwards, Christians admitted the existence of guardian angels. While in the East they were attributed only to the baptised, in the West it was maintained that every man was assigned one from the moment he was born. This latter doctrine has persisted to this day in the Catholic Church. Even the inhabitants of the Orinoco, once reputed to be the most ferocious of all savages, each have a guardian angel.

While the tradition may be very ancient, the official cult of guardian angels among Catholics came fairly late—and the more the Protestants were to condemn it, the more it would flourish. It came into being under the aegis of the blessed François d'Estaing, Bishop of Rodez, who dedicated a chapel to them in his cathedral, where, with the blessing of Pope Leo X, he was to celebrate a first Mass in their honour on 3 June 1529. The congregation was so vast that the bishop ended up celebrating his Mass outside, against a backdrop of mountains. In 1670, Clement X imposed the Feast of the Holy Guardian Angels on the universal Church, but it was only in 1853 that the Council of Rheims fixed its date at 2 October.

But guardian angels needed no consecration to be popular, least of all with preachers. Bossuet[2] devoted one of his enthusiastic marathon sermons to them: '"They are the ambassadors of God to man, they are the ambassadors of man to God. What a marvel!" comments Saint Bernard.

1 Matthew xviii, 10.
2 French orator, churchman, historian and political thinker (1627–1704).

Christians, can you believe it? They are not only the angels of God, but the angels of man as well.'

'The guardian angel is a good counsellor. He intercedes with God in our favour; he helps us in our needs; he keeps us safe from accidents,' said Pope John XXIII,[1] who even used his own as an alarm clock. This close guard performs no less than six functions for the individual to whom he is assigned: he wards off dangers which threaten both his body and his soul; he cracks down on demons; he presents his prayers to God, and prays to God for him; he encourages him to do good; and, finally, he brings him back on course when he strays from the straight and narrow.

This last task would seem a far cry from the 'cute' image of him that lacy first communions used to convey. Saint Frances of Rome (1384–1440), for example, had a particularly spirited guardian angel who would not let her get away with anything, even in public. One evening, she was giving a dinner party for the cream of Roman society in her husband Lorenzo's palazzo; the conversation was becoming delightfully frivolous and the tittle-tattle was in full swing. Either tired, or bored with the presence of table companions of a certain age, the young mistress of the house (she was seventeen) let her feelings be known. Her attitude did not please her guardian angel one bit. Suddenly the guests were stunned by the sound of a sharp slap on Frances' face—and immediately saw its effect on her flaming cheek. Her good angel had hit her!

A guardian angel does not abandon his man at the point of death; according to Melanie de La Salette, he waits patiently for his soul to emerge from purgatory,[2] if that is where it has gone. Such professional conscientiousness is impossible to fault.

---

1 26 December 1962.
2 Where the souls of the just are purified before attaining paradise, to which only saints have direct access.

INTERNATIONAL DEFENCE

Airborne troops

Who would have thought, from those chubby-cheeked little cherubs on greeting cards, that angels are first and foremost the militia of the armies of heaven? These redoubtable warriors are not averse, from time to time, to earthly combat, and their efficacy is no longer in doubt: 'And it came to pass that night, that the angel of the Lord went out, and smote in the camp of the Assyrians an hundred fourscore and five thousand: and when they arose early in the morning, behold, they were all dead corpses.'[1]

Cavalry

Angels can also ride. In battle the Prophet Mohammed, who often rode to combat on a white camel, received reinforcements of three thousand angel-cavalrymen at Badr, the Muslims' first great victory in the second year of the Hegira (AD 624), when they were fighting with only 313 men against a thousand better-equipped Meccans. It is reported that these angel-cavalrymen wore yellow and white turbans and that their horses were roans.

Admin

Each nation has a protecting angel.[2] Michael is Israel's, which he defends with his legions of angels. But when his people turn away from God he steps aside, leaving the angels of other nations to attack them and even transmit to them fevers and pestilence. These other angels are themselves broken 'with a rod of iron' the moment Israel returns to the Lord.[3]

---

1 II Kings xix, 35.
2 Daniel x, 21.
3 Psalms ii, 9.

Recruitment office

Michael is also the protector of France. This is why he appeared, accompanied by Saint Catherine and Saint Margaret, both virgin-martyrs, to the young Joan of Arc, urging her to go and find the Dauphin, the future Charles VII, and save the country. Then, after her triumph, her burning and her canonisation, Joan ranked with the two saints inasmuch as she was a virgin-martyr, and with the archangel in her capacity of patron saint of France.

Heavy artillery

As a Jewish angel can accomplish only one mission at a time, the Talmud identifies thus the three angels who visited Abraham in the Plains of Mamre: Raphael, angel of healing, who comes to heal up his late circumcision; Michael, protector of Israel, who announces to him the birth of Isaac; and Gabriel, angel of strength, who tells him that he is going to destroy Sodom and Gomorrah.

There is no eyewitness to this annihilation: Lot's wife, who turned round for a quick look, was immediately transformed into a pillar of salt. She had been warned! The Bible records that 'the Lord rained upon Sodom and upon Gomorrah brimstone and fire from the Lord out of heaven; And he overthrew those cities, and all the plain, and all the inhabitants of the cities, and that which grew upon the ground.'[1] The following morning Abraham saw something 'like the smoke from a furnace' rise from the ruins.

The explanation comes much later, when Mohammed asks the angel Gabriel to demonstrate his strength: 'On my wings I have raised the towns of the people of Lot,' he replies, 'so high into the air that the inhabitants of the sky could hear their cock crowing; then I brought them down to earth', as Toufic Fahd notes.

What awesome simplicity.

---

1 Genesis xix, 24–5.

TERRITORIAL SECURITY

Planet control

It is vital that the Earth should turn: this too is a job for the angels. In Jewish mysticism, the stars receive their instructions from them.

The angels who inhabit the planetary spheres are responsible for their rotation: they are the mechanics of the heavens. Many astronomers, notably Kepler,[1] upheld the theory of the *angelus rector*, of the angel who directs the sun, because there had to be an intelligence to calculate its orbit and maintain it there. As for the Polish canon, Nicholas Copernicus, after his demise he left a heliocentric universe in which man on his small planet Earth was becoming more insignificant, while the planets continued to reside on crystalline spheres, driven along by angels.

The angels in charge of world order are called by Muslims *Al-muwakkalūn*. And as far as poetry goes, Islam will always have the last word: 'The sun is entrusted to the care of nine angels, who throw snow upon it every day; otherwise it could burn everything.'[2]

Traffic control

Balaam the soothsayer provoked God's anger by tagging along after the princes of Moab. So God posted an angel across his path, with a sword in his hand by way of a traffic-control baton. When Balaam's ass saw the angel she left the road to avoid him, but Balaam, not being a very enlightened soothsayer, had seen nothing at all and gave his mount a severe thrashing to teach her to walk straight. Further on, as the path grew narrower, the ass walked so close to the wall to avoid the angel again that she scraped Balaam's foot against the rock. A second beating ensued. The third time the angel appeared, the path was so narrow that the ass,

1 Johannes Kepler (1571–1630), German, author of *Mysterium Cosmographicum*.
2 Tabarnī, after Abi Ouamana.

being unable to continue, lay down on the ground. Balaam, collapsing with her, was furious, and beat the animal again.

Then God made the ass talk, and insult Balaam: 'What have I done unto thee, that thou hast smitten me these three times?'[1] With not a flicker of a smile, Balaam replied that she was making fun of him. Then he saw the angel, who advised him to thank his ass: if she had not turned away from him, he would have killed him with his sword.

What a lesson it was for a deviant prophet to see God talking to him through the mouth of an ass and through the eyes of that same creature seeing an angel, where there was nothing but the dusty road. And to think some people claim He has no sense of humour!

Veterinary services

So angels have a feeling for animals, even wild ones. This was verified when, in a somewhat unfriendly fashion, King Darius sent Daniel into the lions' den:

> Then the king arose very early in the morning, and went in haste unto the den of lions.
>
> And when he came to the den, he cried with a lamentable voice unto Daniel: and the king spake and said to Daniel, O Daniel, servant of the living God, is thy God, whom thou servest continually, able to deliver thee from the lions?
>
> Then said Daniel unto the king, O king, live for ever.
>
> My God hath sent his angel, and hath shut the lions' mouths, that they have not hurt me.[2]

However, the lions were still a bit peckish, for when Darius sent those who had slandered Daniel, along with their wives and children, into their den the lions 'brake all their bones in pieces or ever they came at the bottom of the den'.[3] The angel-lion-tamer had gone to perform elsewhere.

1 Numbers xxii, 28.
2 Daniel vi, 19–22.
3 Daniel vi, 24.

Firemen

As fire-fighters, not only can angels dispense with asbestos
suits, but they are capable of being their own fire protection.
Take the example of Ananias, Mishael and Azariah (Shad-
rach, Meshach and Abed-nego), who were thrown into a
furnace by King Nebuchadnezzar. 'But the angel of the Lord
came down into the furnace beside Azariah and his companions; he drove the flames of the fire outwards, and fanned
in to them, in the heart of the furnace, a coolness such as
wind and dew will bring, so that the fire did not even touch
them or cause them any pain or distress.'[1]

Evidently, the king found this bizarre. 'Then Nebuchadnezzar . . . said unto his counsellors, Did not we cast three men
bound into the midst of the fire? They answered and said
unto the king, True, O king. He answered and said, Lo, I see
four men loose, walking in the midst of the fire, and they
have no hurt; and the form of the fourth is like the Son of
God'.[2] When they emerged, our three fellows had not the
slightest smell of burning on them—and the fourth, the duty
fireman, had literally flown away.

Fanfares and serenades

Everyone knows that up there in heaven the angels sing and
their wings hum. At the end of time, they also have to awaken
the dead with the sound of trumpets: 'And he shall send his
angels with a great sound of a trumpet, and they shall gather
together his elect from the four winds, from one end of heaven
to the other.'[3]

In Islam, this role is performed by a single gigantic angel—
Israfil. Covered with tongues and curly hair, he has four
wings: the first spreads over the East, the second over the
West; he covers himself with the third, while the fourth serves
as a veil separating him from the majesty of God. He always

1 Daniel iii, 49–50. These verses are taken from the Jerusalem Bible, published and
copyright © 1966, 1967 and 1968 by Darton Longman and Todd Ltd. and Doubleday,
a division of Random House, Inc., and used by permission of the publishers.
2 Daniel iii, 24–5.
3 Matthew xxiv, 31.

has a trumpet at his lips, ready to blow as soon as God gives him the command. One blast on his trumpet will awaken the dead in their tombs. In the meantime, when he looks at hell Israfil suffers and weeps so violently that his tears threaten to flood the earth.

If angels love brass instruments, they are equally fond of strings. St Francis of Assisi confided one day to Brother Leo that an angel with a violin had appeared to him. He had lightly touched the strings only once but the sound was so lovely, he said, that 'had the angel drawn the bow lower down, the unbearable sweetness of it would have caused my soul to leave my body.'

CATERING SERVICE

If the angels sometimes do the cooking in heaven, it is only natural that on Earth they should wait at table.

Home delivery

The prophet Elijah fled from the deadly anger of the infamous queen Jezebel into the desert, where, at the end of his tether, filled with despair and wanting only to die, he finally fell asleep. 'And . . . behold, then an angel touched him, and said unto him, Arise and eat. And he looked, and, behold, there was a cake baken on the coals, and a cruse of water at his head. And he did eat and drink.'[1] This was, of course, very basic fare, but adapted for country living and served hot. With gentle insistence, the angel made Elijah eat a second time. And sustained by this food, whose energy content must have been surprisingly high, Elijah was able to spend forty days in the desert without taking another bite.

It was also after Jesus had spent forty days and forty nights fasting in the desert, and had come face to face with Satan, that the angels came to serve him a meal.[2] There had been no need for his mother, on the other hand, to go to such extremes in order to benefit from the service: according to

1 I Kings xix, 5–6.
2 Matthew iv, 11.

the Apocrypha, when Mary was a young girl in the Temple, 'every day she ate only the food that she received from the hand of the angel'.[1]

Takeaway

Even more extraordinary is that an angel can transport a cook more than six hundred kilometres over desolate terrain without the food getting cold.

> Now there was in Jewry a prophet called Habbacuc, who had made pottage, and had broken bread in a bowl, and was going to the fields for to bring it to the reapers.
>
> But the angel of the Lord said unto Habbacuc, Go, carry the dinner that thou hast into Babylon unto Daniel, who is in the lions' den.
>
> And Habbacuc replied, I never saw Babylon; neither do I know where the den is.
>
> Then the angel of the Lord took him by the crown and bare him by his hair of his head, and through the vehemency of his spirit set him down in Babylon over the den.
>
> And Habbacuc cried, saying, O Daniel, Daniel, take this dinner which God hath sent thee.
>
> And Daniel said, Thou hast remembered me, O God; neither hast thou forsaken them that seek thee, and love thee.
>
> So Daniel did eat and the angel of the Lord set Habbacuc in his own place again.[2]

Aids to digestion

Not only does the angel deliver food, but he also aids digestion. We do not give enough thought to the fact that angels can walk about in our insides. For Muslims, this is certainly

---

1 Pseudo-Matthew vi, 3; Proto-Gospel of James, viii, 1.
2 'The History of the Destruction of Bel and the Dragon', 33–9.

what happens. The assimilation of food necessitates the intervention of no more and no less than seven angels.

The first carries the food into the body, because it cannot do it on its own; the second keeps it in place during the breaking-down process; the third gives it the form of blood; the fourth removes waste; the fifth supervises its distribution between the bones, the flesh and the veins; the sixth assimilates it; the seventh ensures that the whole system works harmoniously, 'for, if, for example, the quantity of food accumulated on the nose of a child were equal to that accumulated on the leg, the nose would expand, cease to be hollow, and the face, along with the whole of creation, would find itself quite changed.'[1] So this angel must take the finest food to the eyelids, the clearest to the pupils, the most solid to the bones, and so on. He is the body's architect.

DAYBOOK

Births

From the moment of conception, the angel operates as a cosmetic surgeon. In fact, says the Talmud,[2] before birth man is pure spirit and knows everything; but at the moment of birth an angel puts his finger on his mouth and he forgets the Torah. The small cleft that runs between our noses and mouths is where the angel put his finger on our infant lips so as to silence us and make us forget about God's secrets.

Marriages

It is often the role of angels to announce an unforeseen and miraculous birth to a sterile woman (such as Sarah and her son Isaac, the wife of Manoah and her Samson) but, in addition, they can also act as go-betweens. In true biblical chic, a plier of this trade is known as a 'paranymph'. Raphael, as we have seen, was given the task of finding a wife for the young Tobias: a girl whose seven previous fiancés had been

---

1 Qazwini, 62s.
2 *Niddah*, 16a, para. 30b.

successively bumped off by the demon Asmodeus. But this was of no importance, because the angel had the answer. Tobias lived happily ever after and had many children.

The angel of God was absolutely not a puritan, nor was he a fan of monogamy—not, at least, in very ancient times, for he procured both Leah and Rachel as wives for Jacob.

And deaths

'And it came to pass, that the beggar died, and was carried by the angels into Abraham's bosom,'[1] says Saint Luke. Angels are also undertakers; or, in more celestial terminology, psychopomps—that is, transporters of souls. 'He sends forth guardians who watch over you and claim your souls without fail when death overtakes you,' says the Koran.[2] These emissaries are the angel of death and his escorts the angels of mercy and punishment.

In Jewish tradition,[3] on the day when King David was due to die the angel of death (*malakh ha-mavet*) could not get near him because he was studying the Torah all the time. The angel then had the idea of shaking the trees outside. Wondering what was happening, King David abandoned his studies and went outside. His foot slipped, and he died.

In Islam, the angel of death is called Azrael (Izrā'īl). This gigantic angel, with his four thousand wings, has as many assistants as he has dying people to contend with. Legend has it that he was a friend of King Solomon, to whom he paid a visit in human form every Thursday. One afternoon, he fixed his gaze for a long time on one of the king's guests. After he had gone, the guest asked the king who his friend was. When he learnt that he was the angel of death he took fright, and so as to escape the angel's clutches he asked Solomon if he could be transported on the wind to the outer confines of India. No sooner said than done. When the angel of death returned to see Solomon the following week, the king pointed out that he had noticed him looking very strangely at

1 Luke xvi, 22.
2 Koran vi, 62.
3 *Shabbat*, 30b.

one of his guests on his last visit. 'In fact,' the angel replied, 'I was astonished to see him here, because I had received the order to seize his soul very soon on the Indian border!'

No one escapes Izrā'īl! Not even Moses, who, however, did defend himself and, it is said, put out one of his eyes— which could not have handicapped him enormously, though, because according to Jewish folklore he is entirely covered in eyes.

Moral: 'When you see a funeral procession pass by, whether it be of a Muslim, a Jew or a Christian, stand up. It is not for the cortege that we should stand, but for the angels accompanying it.'[1]

---

1 Abū Dāwūd in *Sunan*.

Chapter Six

Plumage and Song

In which we move up a rung to investigate angels' heavenly appearance, their size and number of wings, their singing and their organisation in heaven; and discover some impressive, not to say terrifying yet likeable, personalities.

The most widespread idea about angels is that they never go anywhere without at least one sturdy pair of wings. However, the Scriptures mention quite a few magnificent angels who have no feathers, and no complexes either.

When the angels come down to Earth to meet humans they are disguised as men, without the feathers. How do they do it? The all-knowing Saint Thomas Aquinas explains it very simply: 'At its ordinary level of expansion, air retains neither shape nor colour; but when it is condensed, it can take on different forms and reflect colours: we see this in clouds. It is when they are in the upper air, therefore, that with God's assistance they form bodies, by solidifying the air through condensation as much as is necessary.'[1] So the bodies that angels assume are formed from a sort of radiant vapour.

As beautiful as an angel

While we cannot vouch for the formula, there is no doubt that it works very well. Angels have the appearance of very handsome, very well dressed, young men. On 1 March 1431, when the judges, with their twisted minds, were pressing Joan of Arc with questions, she answered with further questions:

1 *Summa Theologiae*, Ia pars, Q. 51, a. 2.

'When Saint Michael appeared to you, was he naked?'
'Do you think God has nothing to clothe him in?'
'Did he have hair?'
'Why would anyone have cut it?'[1]

She refused to add the smallest detail. Scarcely any exist,
except in the Book of Daniel; it was Daniel who, after three
weeks of fasting on the banks of the Tigris, saw 'a certain
man clothed in linen, whose loins were girded with fine gold
of Uphaz: His body also was like the beryl, and his face as
the appearance of lightning, and his eyes as lamps of fire,
and his arms and his feet like in colour to polished brass,
and the voice of his words like the voice of a multitude.'[2]

Angels have such a reputation among women for their
handsome looks that they can cause accidents in the home.
Even when the supposed apparition is only a man, it is just
as well not to be peeling fruit at the time: 'When they saw
him, they were amazed at him and cut their hands, exclaim-
ing: "God preserve us! This is no mortal, but a gracious
angel." '[3]

The Bible is very precise on the fate that threatened such
pretty young men in Sodom. This episode also features in the
Koran, where Lot, the one just man in Sodom, only has to
see the angels arriving to foresee the lust they will arouse
amongst his fellow citizens. So he offers them his own daughters instead.

When Our messengers came to Lot, he grew anxious
about them, for he was powerless to offer them protection. 'This is indeed a day of woe,' he said.

His people, long addicted to evil practices, came run-
ning towards him. 'My people,' he said, 'here are my
daughters: surely they are more wholesome to you. Fear
God, and do not shame me by insulting my guests. Is
there not one right-minded man among you?'[4]

1 Quoted in *Jeanne d'Arc*, Régine Pernoud and M.-V. Clin, Fayard.
2 Daniel x, 5–6.
3 Koran xii, 31.
4 Koran xi, 77–8.

It was a day of woe, indeed ... having pulled the wool over their eyes, the angels got away from the Sodomites. As for the daughters of Lot, they suffered a somewhat bizarre fate, sexually. Since they were the only ones, with their father, to escape the destruction of the city, they ended up getting him drunk and violating him in order to acquire offspring from the very man who had so obligingly offered them, though in vain, for a gang-bang. It seems that the laws of hospitality—and the duty to perpetuate the species—were more sacred, at that time, than others. Bourgeois morality came much later.

One thing is certain, however: these particular handsome angels did not have wings. Zealous and wingless is what they were. We know this primarily because the Scriptures and, in particular, Daniel, who is so precise, make no mention of wings, but also because wings would have hampered them. If the angel who came to announce the birth of Samson to Manoah, for example, 'ascended in the flame of the altar',[1] it was precisely because he had no wings; anyway, Manoah did not identify him as an angel. Nor did anyone, throughout his travels with the young Tobias, unmask Raphael, and it would have been difficult for him to pass unnoticed, wearing wings, even folded ones, in the midst of a wedding feast! And then how is it that Jacob's angels insist on going up and down a ladder,[2] if they can fly? While it may be true that swallows can leap from one electric cable to another without spreading their wings, the argument might seem a little far-fetched. There is nothing, either, to indicate that Gabriel had wings when he came to see Mary. And the angel that the holy women meet near Jesus' tomb is 'a young man ... clothed in a long white garment'.[3] No question of wings.

Furthermore, in Christian art angels are not seen wearing wings until the beginning of the fourth century. But there was another reason for this: many pagan gods had them, and it was essential to differentiate between the two. In the Rome of the epic film, with its lions hungry for freshly baptised

1 Judges xiii, 20.
2 Genesis xxviii, 12.
3 Mark xvi, 5.

flesh, Cupid, god of love (Eros in ancient Greece), Victoria (Nikē, victory), symbol of the power of the emperors, Mercury (Hermes), messenger of the gods, and other infamous idols—all these were shown with wings. So the early Christians had featherless angels right up until Emperor Constantine's conversion to Christianity. After the Edict of Milan in 313, when at last they believed themselves safe from wild beasts and irritating confusions, they allowed their angels to grow wings so large that they came to symbolise their wearers in the same way that haloes symbolise saints. It took all the affable impudence of Michelangelo, in Rome, to dare depict in his *Last Judgement* a beardless Christ, saints with no underpants and angels without feathers. Some of the popes put the pants back on the men, but no one dared give those unconventional angels wings again.

The very first angels' wings were painted white in the West and red in the East: the colours of the wine used to celebrate Mass and of liturgical vestments—white as symbolic of purity in the West, and red as symbolic of the fire of enlightenment in the East.

And yet they can fly . . .

But where did their wings come from?

According to the Koran, they derive from the angels' actual appearance in heaven, a world naturally invisible to men: 'Praise be to God, Creator of the heavens and the earth! He sends forth the angels as His messengers, with two, three or four pairs of wings. He multiplies His creatures according to His will.'[1] However, the Prophet Mohammed himself saw the angel Gabriel only once or twice in his heavenly aspect, his feet on the ground and his head in the sky and his several hundreds of pairs of wings with their dazzling feathers obscuring the whole horizon. When he saw him, Mohammed fell to the ground in a faint, stiff as a corpse. The angel, as he brought him round, commented: 'What would you do if you saw Israfïl [the angel with the 'Resurrection trumpet'], with his head under the throne and his feet on the seventh

1 Koran xxxv, 1.

earth, yet who before the majesty of God is as tiny as a bullfinch?"[1]

Since angels do not set out to make prophets swoon, Gabriel got into the habit of coming to see Mohammed in the guise of Dihya al-Kalbī, a handsome young man of medium build who wore green clothes and a silk turban and rode a horse or a mule. In those times and in that place, his appearance went quite unremarked. The angel, celestial dandy that he was, was always in the latest fashion.

Those beautiful angels who are tactful enough to visit men in human guise form the minority of an infinitely larger angelic world. And that world is well guarded. After He had banished Adam, God 'placed at the east of the garden of Eden Cherubims, and a flaming sword which turned every way, to keep the way of the tree of life'.[2] These cherubs, the angelic sentries of the Kingdom of God, have wings. God Himself says so when he tells Moses to construct a mobile sanctuary, which is where His presence will reside among His people in the desert. His orders are very specific. He wants the Ark of the Covenant, a gold-decorated acacia wood chest destined to contain the tablets of the Law, to be surmounted with a pure gold covering, the mercy-seat,[3] itself flanked by two cherubim at each end. The Law contained in the Ark forbade all making of images, and God is well placed to know this, since it was He Himself who said: 'Thou shalt not make unto thee any graven image, nor any likeness of any thing that is in heaven above, or that is in the earth beneath, or that is in the water under the earth.'[4] However, this is what He ordered Moses to do:

> And thou shalt make two cherubims of gold, of beaten work . . . in the two ends of the mercy seat . . .
> And the cherubims shall stretch forth their wings on high, covering the mercy seat with their wings, and their

1 Ka'b al-Ahbār.
2 Genesis iii, 24.
3 Regarded as the resting-place of God, His throne. In French, *propitiatoire*: the purpose of the 'propitiation' was to win God's favour through a sacrifice or gift. Trans.
4 Exodus xx, 4.

faces shall look one to another: toward the mercy seat shall the faces of the cherubims be.

And thou shalt put the mercy seat above upon the ark; and in the ark thou shalt put the testimony that I shall give thee.

And there I will meet with thee, and I will commune with thee from above the mercy seat, from between the two cherubims which are upon the ark of the testimony, of all things which I will give thee in commandment unto the children of Israel.[1]

This is all Him. But didn't He also forbid murder, then command Abraham to sacrifice his son in His honour, but then stop him from doing it? He is a jealous God (this He readily admits), and so He forbids representations that might lead to idolatry—but commissions representations of cherubim that will be turned to face the empty space of His Word. In doing this, He wants to signal to His listeners that, from lost paradise, He is continuing to send out transmissions. Or that He is, Himself, unrepresentable—in fact, hovering between two representations: the God who is always invisible, but more than ever, the God who is always audible—'Hear, O Israel' . . . The sanctuary will be God's radio in the desert.

As counterparts to the heavenly cherubim, these earthly ones, who indicate in their gaze the source of their prophetic inspiration, have the form of winged men. Much later, when Solomon built a permanent temple in Jerusalem—which his father King David had conquered around 1000 BC—to shelter God's Ark which, along with His people, had ceased to be nomadic, he made two cherubim of wild olivewood. Each of their wings was six cubits (2.3 metres) long, and 'stretched forth . . . so that the wing of the one touched the one wall, and the wing of the other cherub touched the other wall; and their wings touched one another in the midst of the house'.[2] Today it is still common to see, on either side of the altar in old Catholic churches, demurely kneeling, modest replicas of

1 Exodus xxv, 18, 20–22.
2 I Kings vi, 27.

these biblical cherubim who, by contrast, always stood. Jewish tradition records, in fact, that since angels have no knee joints they have to stand upright all the time.

The choir of seraphim

Thanks to a particularly inspired prophet named Isaiah, more than two centuries after the death of Solomon the existence of other angels was discovered in Jerusalem. In 740 BC, writes Isaiah,

> In the year that king Uzziah died I saw also the Lord sitting upon a throne, high and lifted up, and his train filled the temple.
>
> Above it stood the seraphims: each one had six wings; with twain he covered his face, and with twain he covered his feet, and with twain he did fly.
>
> And one cried unto another, and said, Holy, holy, holy, is the Lord of hosts: the whole earth is full of his glory.[1]

The seraphim cover their faces with two wings because they are in the presence of God; 'with [two wings] he covered his feet' is a classic euphemism for sex organs (again!); and with two wings, they flew. These hexapterous angels can often be seen under the cupolas of Orthodox churches. In Greece they look like those marvellous twisted doughnuts, and in Russia like somewhat dishevelled stars. It was a crucified seraph who stigmatised Saint Francis of Assisi (1186–1226) on Mount Alverno two years before he died. In the Louvre there is a painting by Giotto based on Saint Bonaventure's account:

> And now he saw, coming down from the sky, a seraph with six wings blazing like fire. He flew speedily to the place where the man of God was standing, and a figure appeared between the wings. It was that of a crucified man, with his hands and feet stretched out and attached

1 Isaiah vi, 1–3.

to a cross. Two wings rose above his head, two others were spread ready for flight, and the last two hid his body.[1]

Even more famous is the statue in the Church of Santa Maria della Vittoria in Rome, where Bernini has encapsulated in marble the ecstasy transmitted to Saint Teresa of Avila (1515–82) by a seraph, even though she mistook this anonymous anthropomorph for another: 'God willed that I saw on my left an angel, in bodily form ... He was not large, but small and very handsome; his glowing face indicated that he belonged to the highest of the hierarchies, that of the spirits burning with love. These are, I think, what are known as cherubim. They did not tell me their names.' She was wrong. These were seraphim: their name comes from the Hebrew *saraf*, meaning 'to burn'. The angel transfixed her 'right through the heart to [her] entrails' with a golden dart that left her 'burning with the most ardent love of God'. The pain was so intense that she trembled, 'but at the same time, the sweetness caused by this incomparable pain was so extreme that my soul longed for it never to end'.[2]

It is hard to know which of the two—her writing or the sculpture—has since given rise to more male fantasy. If only men knew how Saint Teresa concluded her account—'I beg the Lord, in his goodness, to deign to favour those who believe I have invented all this with the real thing for themselves'—they would be knees down on their prie-dieux forthwith.

As well as a pictorial and a sculptural heritage, seraphim also have a musical one. In fact, their 'cry'[3] has been adopted in Church liturgy under the name of *qedusha* in Hebrew, *sanctus* in Latin, and *trisagion*[4] in Greek. *Qadosh, qadosh, qadosh, Adonai tsebaot* means 'Holy, holy, holy, Lord God of Hosts'—that is, of angels, for the armies of God are heavenly ones. In Jewish tradition, the angels sing the *qedusha* at night, and keep quiet during the day when men

1 Saint Bonaventure, *Legenda major*, xiii, 2.
2 Teresa of Avila, *Life*, xxix, 13.
3 The Hebrew *qara* means 'utter the sacred word in a loud voice'.
4 From *tris*, 'three', and *hagios* 'holy'.

111

take their turn to pray.[1] Earth and heaven harmonise. Among Christians, the earthly liturgy becomes part of the heavenly liturgy, which has continued uninterrupted since Christ's Ascension. Furthermore, the angels go to Mass with humans, and during the Eucharist 'the whole of the sanctuary and the space around the altar are filled with the celestial armies in honour of him who is on the altar, just as one sees soldiers behaving in the presence of the king,' wrote Saint John Chrysostom. Mosques, too, at the time of prayer, attract clouds of travelling angels.

A God borne by angels

Isaiah had seen God on his throne, and almost 150 years later, during the exodus to Babylon, the prophet Ezekiel would see the base of the throne—it was a chariot. In 592 BC the Temple of Solomon was destroyed, and God, once more in nomadic mode, was on the road with His people. First, Ezekiel saw the column of cloud and fire which accompanied the Jews as they came out of Egypt, and which Isaiah had seen in the temple of Jerusalem. Later, the Talmudists would call it the *Shekhinah*, the divine presence. Then . . .

> Out of the midst thereof came the likeness of four living creatures. And this was their appearance; they had the likeness of a man.
>
> And every one had four faces, and every one had four wings.
>
> And their feet were straight feet; and the sole of their feet was like the sole of a calf's foot: and they sparkled like the colour of burnished brass.
>
> And they had the hands of a man under their wings on their four sides; and they four had their faces and their wings.
>
> Their wings were joined one to another; they turned not when they went; they went every one straight forward.
>
> As for the likeness of their faces, they four had the

1 *Hagigah*, 12b.

face of a man, and the face of a lion, on the right side; and they four had the face of an ox on the left side; they four also had the face of an eagle.

Thus were their faces; and their wings were stretched upward; two wings of every one were joined one to another, and two covered their bodies.

And they went every one straight forward: whither the spirit was to go, they went; and they turned not when they went.

At what speed? The 'living creatures ran and returned as the appearance of a flash of lightning.'[1] The terrifying appearance of these strange angels, half-human, half-beast, has been explained by the presence of statues of the Babylonian religious cult that the Jews in exile would have been able to observe at the time. But the invisible world, even though described, remains nonetheless *un*visualisable.

And this is not the whole story, either. Beside these living creatures (*hayyoth*) with four faces there are wheels (*ofanim*), which are also angels and whose task it is to accompany the living creatures on their travels: 'When they went, they went upon their four sides: and they turned not when they went. As for their rings, they were so high that they were dreadful; and their rings were full of eyes round about them four.'[2] Above the living creatures and the wheels is 'the likeness of a throne' made of sapphire, and above this 'the appearance of a man', encircled by fire and by a rainbow glow: the glory of God.

All this has a meaning: to do with God, primarily. Why do the Scriptures often ascribe to Him a human body, a face, arms, feet and hands and even a particularly threatening finger when, as no one doubts, He is pure spirit? Remember Voltaire's ironic remark: 'If God made man in his image, man has well and truly given it back to him.' In fact, though, an ancient midrash says almost exactly the opposite: that these images do not derive from man's projection of his own image, but from God's desire to borrow His creatures'

1 Ezekiel i, 5–12, 14.
2 Ezekiel I, 17–18.

vocabulary in order to explain His relationship with the world.

As for the strange angels' chariot, it is at the root of the first Jewish mysticism, dating back to long before the Cabbala and known as *merkabah* mysticism. The *merkabah* was the chariot that Ezekiel describes. These mystics succeed in contemplating God, beyond human reason, and seeing the invisible. Their experience remains almost incommunicable; nevertheless, the fundamentals of their approach can be understood. In order to reach God, the *merkabah* mystics hitch a ride on Ezekiel's chariot. For them, this vision expresses the four spiritual worlds that correspond to the four letters of God's name—YHVH, Jehovah—according to the verse, 'Even every one that is called by my name: for I have created him for my glory, I have formed him; yea, I have made him.'[1] Here they find four worlds between God and man: the worlds of glory, creation, formation and fabrication; and to get close to God they have to ascend, in reverse order, from the world of fabrication to the world of glory.

At the lowest level then, the world of fabrication (*assiya*), the physical world in which we live, corresponds to the *ofanim*: the wheels in Ezekiel's vision. Above, the world of formation (*yetsira*), the world of the angels, establishes the link between God and our world; it corresponds to the *hayyoth*, the living creatures with four faces. Yet higher up is the world of creation (*beriya*), situated 'above the vault over the heads of the angels', where the throne is. God sits there, or rather He inclines towards us. And finally there is the highest world of all, that of the Glory of God (*atsilut*) which, for Ezekiel, is incarnated in the Man seated on the throne. Here we acknowledge 'divine emanations' (*sephiroth*), for 'love is His right hand; power, His left hand; glory is His body; victory and splendour are His two feet . . . Wisdom is His brain; understanding, His heart . . . and the absolute crown is the place where the *tefillin* rest.'[2]

Although we can trace the path that the *merkabah* mystics

---

1 Isaiah xliii, 7.

2 Introduction to *Tikkun Zohar*. *Tefillin* are phylacteries, small leather boxes containing four biblical passages that Jews wear on the forehead and left arm in order to say their morning prayers.

take, it is difficult to know how they reach their objective. Aryeh Kaplan, a specialist on the subject, suggests that they may use certain verses of seventy-two letters:[1] for example, the one that introduces Ezekiel's text—'Now it came to pass in the thirtieth year, in the fourth month, in the fifth day of the month, as I was among the captives by the river of Chebar, that the heavens were opened, and I saw visions of God'— and that they repeat these verses like mantras so as to see the heavens opening. Mysticism and mystery, surely, have the same root.

Christian artists, great painters and sculptors of angels, would be stumped when faced with Ezekiel's vision, for the chariot is too powerful, too full of movement, to be frozen in an image. A bas-relief in Amiens Cathedral shows Ezekiel pensive, his head resting on his hand, contemplating two poor little wheels locked into one another—as though he himself despairs of this pathetic depiction.

On the other hand, those same artists present an odd sort of fate for the *hayyoth*, the living creatures, the angels with four heads who uphold God's throne and that the Bible, undoubtedly because of their hooves, translates as 'beasts'. In fact, Saint John, like Ezekiel before him, saw them and recalled them in his Apocalypse.

The metamorphosis of the living creatures

Over the next six hundred and fifty years, the living creatures changed. By the end of the first century AD they were no longer quadricephalous—each now had one head. They had acquired their multiple eyes from the wheels that had disappeared from the now useless chariot:

> And before the throne there was a sea of glass like unto crystal: and in the midst of the throne, and round about the throne, were four beasts full of eyes before and behind.

---

1 Another way of 'counting' God's name, which in Hebrew is written with the letters *yod*, *he*, *vav*, *he*, transcribed as YHVH: if Y=10, H=5, V=6, then Y+YH+YHV+YHVH = 72.

And the first beast was like a lion, and the second beast like a calf, and the third beast had a face as a man, and the fourth beast was like a flying eagle.

And the four beasts had each of them six wings about him.[1]

In the second century, Saint Irenaeus recognised the four evangelists in these four beasts. To this interpretation two more were added, and made such an impact that they would feature around Christ on the portals of all the medieval churches. By the twelfth century, the four beasts symbolised simultaneously Jesus Christ, the virtues of the chosen ones, and the evangelists. First, Christ: the man is the Incarnation—'in Jesus God was made man'; the calf is the Passion, in which Christ himself becomes the sacrificial animal; the lion is the Resurrection, for it was thought at the time that lions slept with their eyes open, as Jesus had in his tomb; finally, the eagle symbolises his Ascension into heaven. The second meaning concerns the virtues: a Christian must be a rational being, ready for sacrifice like the calf, fearless like the lion, and capable of looking eternity in the face, as the eagle does the sun.

Finally, the evangelists themselves: Saint Matthew has man as his sign, because his gospel begins with Jesus' human genealogy; Saint Mark has the lion—he opens his gospel with the voice of the prophet crying in the wilderness; Saint Luke has the calf, or ox, since his introduction recalls Zacharias' sacrifice; and finally Saint John has the eagle, the only creature to look directly at the sun, for his gospel opens with an evocation of God himself.

Today, only this last interpretation—originally the first— remains, and the evangelists are always depicted accompanied by their heavenly beast. This interpretation is in current use; it can explain to the Japanese, for example, why there is a winged lion in St Mark's Square in Venice. And Tintin himself would never have found Red Rackham's treasure buried under the 'cross of the eagle', had he not been able to identify

1 Revelation iv, 6–8.

in the eagle the statue of Saint John hidden among the bric-à-brac at the Loiseau Brothers' in Moulinsart.

Islam also recognises the living creatures: the Koran calls them angel throne-bearers (*Hamalat al-'arsh*) and says that there will be eight of them on the Day of Judgement.[1] In the meantime there are four, as in the Old Testament and the Apocalypse, and they are also presented as a man, a bull, a lion and an eagle.[2] According to Muslim tradition, they intercede on behalf of earthly creatures for their food: the first on behalf of man; the second on behalf of beasts of burden; the third, wild animals; and the fourth, all feathered creatures.

Two are situated under God's 'right foot' and the other two under his 'left foot'; the throne rests on their backs. And the angels nearest God must be of cosmic proportions, because when Mikā'il (the archangel Michael) asked God for permission to circle the throne, he walked for twelve thousand years without ever reaching one of its pillars.[3] Then he stopped, exhausted. To be more precise, we know that one of their feet was equivalent to seven thousand years of walking. This unit of measurement, which precedes our light-years, might suggest that, if we are talking about walking at a moderate pace day and night, one of these angels' feet would be about 1,634 billion kilometres. By comparison, an angel of a much inferior rank taken at random from Jewish literature—Sandalfon, for example—who is considered big because he outstrips his companions by five hundred years (equivalent to 234 million kilometres), would not even reach the ankle of these gigantic angel throne-bearers! As proof of their gigantic size, Muslims classify angels into three main groups: angels of the throne, heavenly angels and earthly angels.[4]

1 'On that day . . . the angels will stand on all its sides with eight of them carrying the throne of your Lord above their heads.' Koran lxix, 17.
2 Qazwini, 56.
3 Qazwini, 54.
4 Ghazālī, *'Ihyā 'ulūm al-dīn* (The Revival of the Religious Sciences), IV, p. 104.

The nine choirs of holy angels

As far as Christians are concerned, Saint John, who saw the beasts, is not the only apostle to have observed the heavens of the first century. There was also Saint Paul, who wrote in his epistle to the Corinthians: 'I knew a man in Christ above fourteen years ago, (whether in the body, I cannot tell; or whether out of the body, I cannot tell: God knoweth;) such an one caught up to the third heaven ... How that he was caught up into paradise, and heard unspeakable words, which it is not lawful for a man to utter.'[1] Saint Paul was talking about himself, of course. But what had he seen? He does not say. However, he alludes in two of his epistles to several sorts of angels which he is happy to list: Thrones, Dominions, Principalities and Powers.[2]

Christians, then, acknowledge the cherubim, found in the Book of Genesis, as guardians of paradise; the singing seraphim with their six wings, revealed by Isaiah; the living creatures, the throne-bearers, who are mentioned by Ezekiel and seen again by Saint John; the angel-messengers, those very handsome young men scattered throughout the Scriptures; and they also know the names of three of the seven archangels—Michael, Gabriel and Raphael. Furthermore, they inherit that enigmatic list of Saint Paul's, and are not too sure what to make of it. At the beginning of the fifth century, Saint Augustine admitted his perplexity: 'I firmly believe that there are in the heavens Thrones, Dominions, Principalities and Powers, terms by which Saint Paul seemingly describes angelic society. I equally believe that these groups differ between themselves; but even though I may well be scorned for confessing it, I declare that I have no knowledge of what they are or in what ways they differ.'

It would be another century before an answer would be found. At the beginning of the sixth century, in fact, a book appeared that would put an end to all these questions: *The Celestial Hierarchy* by Dionysius the Areopagite. Everyone knows who this Dionysius (also known as Denys) was: he

1 II Corinthians xii, 2, 4.
2 Colossians i, 16; Ephesians i, 21.

features in the Acts of the Apostles as an Athenian philosopher converted by Saint Paul,[1] who had told him all about his journey to the third heaven. Alleluia! At last! No sooner had Dionysius' hierarchy been adopted in the East than it was taught by Pope Gregory I in the West—though it did not really take root here until the ninth century, when it was translated into Latin. Then in the thirteenth century it would be thoroughly digested in the great craw of Saint Thomas Aquinas.[2]

Here, then, are the nine choirs of Christian angels, ranked according to a triple hierarchy of three spheres set between God and mankind.

Right at the top, near God, is the first sphere of perfection, the world of the spirit, which consists of seraphim, cherubim and Thrones. The seraphim[3] burn with the love of God, 'purify the others and illuminate them through the fire of their charity', according to Saint Thomas. The cherubim[4] contemplate the wisdom of God, the beauty and order of things. The Thrones serve as God's seat; placed high above the Earth, they receive God and carry Him to the lower orders.

The second sphere, that of enlightenment and of the world of the soul, links the first world with the third: it has no direct contact with either God or man. Receiving the divine light, it animates and orders the world, which it clothes in beauty. It consists of Dominions, Virtues and Powers. Freed of all servitude, the Dominions rush headlong towards a resemblance to the Master; the Virtues are 'an heroic and unshakeable force'. Those known as Powers imitate divine power and establish the orders of the level below.

The third sphere, that of purification or of the material world, is in contact with mankind. It comprises messengers and guardians: Principalities, archangels and angels. The Principalities have the power of command: they obey the angels above, and lead those below. The archangels,

---

1 Acts xvii, 34.
2 *Summa Theologiae*, Q. 108.
3 *Saraf* means 'to burn'.
4 Meaning 'the spreading of knowledge', according to an unproven etymology attributed to Severus of Antioch.

angel-princes, 'announce great things', according to Saint Gregory. Finally the angels, last in the hierarchy, initiate men into the divine mysteries.

The nine choirs of angels are present on all the cathedrals, in the form of nine luminous circles whose brightness increases the closer they get to the divine source of light. At Chartres on the south doorway, seraphim and cherubim, those closest to God, carry flames and balls of fire; in the East, seraphim have three pairs of red wings and cherubim four blue wings. Thrones take the form of fiery, winged wheels studded with eyes, and Dominions that of women, each with helmet and sword; Virtues, who are very wise, have each a book in their hands, while Principalities adopt a martial stance. Archangels are distinguished from the rest: Michael carries a spear; Gabriel, the messenger, a lantern; and Raphael, the healer, a pot of ointment.

These representations are mostly medieval. After the Renaissance, Christians had become humanists and showed only the last choirs of the last hierarchy—those angels and archangels who came to care for them. As guardian angels, thurifers or deacons, they are sometimes lost in the smiling crowd of chubby little putti with their children's faces. The only one to linger on is the strong personality of Michael, with his dragon pinned under his foot.

It was only at the very end of the nineteenth century that people noticed, by studying Dionysius' language and concepts, that his Neoplatonic vocabulary was anachronistic in relation to the saint that he claimed to be: his was indeed an apocryphal work, one of the pseudepigrapha. And so Saint Dionysius the Areopagite, the great organiser of the Christian heavens, was rebaptised pseudo-Dionysius or pseudo-Denys, in the manner of pseudo-Enoch, father of Jewish angelology. Though he was demoted to his true identity, that of fifth-century philosopher, it was nonetheless conceded that he had married Greek and Christian thought quite brilliantly. But was the Baptistery in Florence to be purged, now, of its heavily feathered seraphim or of its Thrones with eyes as big as saucers?

There was not a moment's hesitation, for the news fell on indifferent ears: who was there who still cared about the celestial hierarchy, anyway? For a long time, no one had been interested in the state of the heavens except in terms of weather forecasts.

Chapter Seven

Footloose in Heaven

*In which we tell of men who were transported live into the
heavens, and what they saw there; follow Mohammed on his
winged mare; investigate the triple careers of the great angels
Michael and Gabriel, in Judaism, Christianity and Islam; and
finish with a nice tale.*

If there are angels who visit Earth, there are also men who
go to heaven—usually, because they are dead. 'And they
haven't come back to tell us about it!' we all chorus, scepti-
cally. 'Neither was there any man known to return from
the grave,' the ungodly were already commenting, and more
elegantly, in the time of King Solomon.[1] Only Enoch and
Elijah went up into heaven without first having died. Some
Jewish traditions actually refer to these men as angels, of
whom Enoch, under the name Metatron, would be the greatest and most powerful: the 'prince of the face'. Nevertheless,
those who claim to have witnessed his exploits come much
too late after his removal heavenwards for their evidence to
qualify as authentic.

It was Christianity that launched the era of returnees from
the dead. But, alas! they remained totally silent about their
impressions of the trip. The ungrateful Lazarus, whom Jesus
brought back to life four days after he had died and who 'by
this time ... stinketh,'[2] gave no press conference after he
emerged from his tomb. He unwrapped the graveclothes from
his ancient corpse without a word. No doubt he folded them
up carefully, so that they could be used again. Lazarus was

1 *The Wisdom of Solomon*, ii, 1.
2 John xi, 39.

just one of the living whose death sentence had been deferred; his momentary resurrection was only a forewarning of a second death, this one inescapable.

Jesus was the first among the dead. According to the Catholic Creed, he 'descended into hell and on the third day rose again from the dead'. He went down into hell to rescue the righteous who had been imprisoned by death—the patriarchs, and first and foremost Adam and Eve, whom his death had freed from their original sin. Scenes such as these can be seen in medieval works of art—but nowhere in the Gospels. Between his Resurrection and his Ascension, Jesus never brought the subject up; he taught his disciples about life; they would see death soon enough, anyway, and in any case he would restore them to life on the Day of Judgement. Moreover, no one among them ever dreamed of questioning him on the subject; the first to take up the issue would come much too late not to be considered suspect himself—apocryphal, in fact. The oldest account of Jesus' trip to the underworld, 'The Questions of Bartholomew', dates from the third century AD.

Among the great voices of monotheism, Mohammed is a case apart: he visited the heavens with the angel Gabriel, and later related his journey to the stunned citizens of Mecca. His spiritual ascension (*mi 'rāj*), which is authenticated in the Koran,[1] is recognised by Muslims and even given a precise date. There are many traditional tales on the subject.[2]

Night ride

On the night of 27 Rajab 620, in Mecca, when he was between waking and sleeping, the Prophet saw three people enter his room, two of whom were the angels Gabriel and Michael. The angel Gabriel, his face ashen and his blond hair floating about him, opened up Mohammed's chest and, with the water of Zemzem, washed away all traces of doubt and falseness from his heart, which he then filled with wisdom

1 Koran xvii, i.
2 In 'Sayings of the Prophet', in the *Sahīh* of Bukhārī, and a commentary on sura lvii by Sheikh Si Hanza Boubakeur, Maisonneuve & Larose.

and faith poured from a golden goblet. Then Gabriel closed up his chest again and, taking Mohammed by the hand, led him to a resplendent white mount, half-mule, half-donkey, but with wings and a woman's head. The mount was known as Burāq (Lightning), and her speed was the speed of light.

And off they flew over the mountains and dunes. They stopped for a while on Mount Sinai, where God spoke to Moses, then at Bethlehem where Jesus was born, and at Hebron where Abraham's tomb was. Finally, in Jerusalem, Mohammed left his mount to ascend into the heavens up a ladder of light, fixed to the very spot where Abraham had almost sacrificed his son; so powerful was their leap that the Prophet's foot and the angel's hand left their imprints in the ground. They will show you the marks, even today, under the golden cupola of the Cathedral of the Rock.

So there they were in the first heaven of the moon and stars, where Mohammed greeted Adam. In the second heaven, he met Jesus and his cousin John the Baptist; in the third, Enoch (Idrīs); in the fourth, Joseph (Yūsuf); in the fifth, Aaron (Hārūn); in the sixth, Moses (Mūsā); and in the seventh heaven, Abraham (Ibrāhīm al-Khalīl), leaning against the hall of the angels, that temple of heaven where, every day, seventy thousand angels enter and leave, never to return. Mohammed was then transported to the lotus jujube tree on the Limit, whose leaves are as broad as elephants' ears and beyond which is the Unknown. Then he crossed endless oceans, zones of fire, of gas, nothingness, light, beauty, perfection, sovereignty, unity. Finally, a mysterious light transported him near the throne of God. He was seized by an icy cold, then felt a radiant sweetness, and God 'revealed to his servant that which he revealed'.[1]

According to tradition, Mohammed did not see God, but sensed Him in his heart. They spoke to each other through the intermediary of an angel. At the end of this exchange, God ordered him to make believers say fifty prayers a day. On the way back, Mohammed again passed by the place where Moses was.

'What duty did he stipulate?' Moses asked.

1 Koran liii, 10.

'Fifty prayers a day!'

'Your nation will never be able to manage it, never. Believe me, I have had experience of men long before you have, and I've had a good deal to put up with from the sons of Israel. Go back to the Lord and ask him to reduce it.'

Mohammed went back, and God let him off ten of the fifty prayers. Moses was waiting for him, and he sent him back to where he'd come from, for the same reason. On each trip, the number of prayers was reduced: forty, thirty, twenty, ten. When Mohammed came back for the fifth time, Moses asked: 'How many prayers?'

'Five.'

'But your nation won't put up with that many! Go back . . .'

'No, I have asked too much of my Lord, and I feel ashamed. This time I accept. I submit to his wishes.'

So Muslims must say five prayers a day; it has always been so.

Mohammed descended the ladder of light again until he reached Jerusalem, then leapt on to his winged mount and returned to Mecca. There, next day, his tale aroused a certain incredulity, not to say hilarity, among his fellow citizens— until they sought out Abu Bakr,[1] who had been to Jerusalem. The description that Mohammed gave him of that city—the Prophet had never been there before mounting Burāq—was so precise that it confounded all those who had been so rude to him.

Islam under Gabriel's wing

In the same way that Ezekiel's vision would give rise to Judaism's first mysticism, that of the *merkabah*, Mohammed's ascension to heaven would give birth to the great Persian mystic belief of the *mi 'rāj* among the Shiite Muslims, whose philosopher is Avicenna and whose poet is Sohravardi, who wrote:

---

1 After the death of the Prophet he would become the first Calif (*khalîfa* means 'successor').

Know that Gabriel has two wings. The right one is of pure light. This whole wing is the unique and pure relationship between Gabriel's being and God. And then there is the left wing. On this wing is a shadowy imprint like the reddish colour of the moon as it rises, or the feet of a peacock. This shadowy imprint is his power-to-be, which has one side turned towards non-being.[1]

So the angel Gabriel has one wing turned towards dawn and the light of the East, and the other towards dusk and the shadows of the West. Since the East symbolises the world of heaven, and the West the earthly world, the mystic pilgrim must, then, 'remove the crimson flush from the angel's wing' by orientating himself—literally, that is, turning to the East whence springs the light. This spiritual Far East is called the Nā-kojā-ābād, the country of 'Nowhere', for the pilgrim will only find it within himself.

On a much more prosaic level, this mythification of the East would explain why Americans have no success in their dealings with Iranian ayatollahs when they talk of 'Western civilisation': long before the birth of capitalism, the West represented for them an image of the worst kind of materialism and of the darkest obscurantism. From where else could the 'Great Satan' have sprung?

Beyond Iran and Shiism, the role of Gabriel (Jibrīl) is of prime importance throughout Islam. Known also as 'the faithful spirit', he is both 'a gracious and mighty messenger, held in honour by the Lord of the Throne',[2] who brought the Koran to Mohammed's heart, and the heavenly guide who led him in his ascension towards God; he is the angel of knowledge and the angel of revelation. His power is cosmic, for it is also Gabriel who made time begin. In fact, when the stars were created, it is said, the moon was as radiant as the sun; and if Gabriel had not dimmed the moon with a beat of his wing, we would not know day from night.[3] Although some mysticisms diverge here, Gabriel traditionally

1 Sohravardi, 'The beating of Gabriel's wings'.
2 Koran lxxxi, 20.
3 Tabarī, commentary.

has six hundred wings, in sets of a hundred, plus two others behind that he uses only to destroy cities—one of his most famous exploits being the annihilation of Sodom and Gomorrah.

Gabriel is 'powerful and mighty', according to the Koran.[1] Here, though, it is only picking up on the word's Hebrew etymology: *guevura* means 'strength' in Hebrew, and Gabriel means 'strength of God'. In the Bible we see him interpreting Daniel's visions; the Talmud links him with the destruction of Sodom, and also credits him with destroying the Temple of Jerusalem and pulling the three young men out of Nebuchadnezzar's furnace. In the Gospel according to Saint Luke, and in the Koran too, he announces the birth of Jesus to Mary. Great angel beloved of Islam and holy archangel of the Christians, Gabriel began his career, like his companion Michael, in Judaism.

FROM ONE MONOTHEISM TO ANOTHER

The great angels' triple careers

Neither Michael nor Gabriel ever served an apprenticeship. They began right away at the highest level. The rabbinical commentaries tell their story as follows: on the first day, once God had created the heavens by spreading light from His garment like a mantle, and had made the Earth from the snow that was under the throne of glory, He gave the world four sides: the East, whence comes the light; the South, whence comes the blessing of the dew and the rain; the West, whence comes darkness; and the North, whence come snow, hail and storms.

On the second day, God created the angels. And here they are, Michael and Gabriel, the very first of the King of Heaven's musketeers:

> Four groups of angels escort and acclaim the Holy One, blessed be He. The first column is that of Michael, who is on His right; the second is that of Gabriel, who is on

---

1 Koran liii, 5.

His left; the third is that of Uriel, who is before Him; the fourth is that of Raphael, who stands behind Him; the *Shekhinah*[1] of the Holy One, blessed be He, is in the centre; exalted and supreme, He is seated on a throne which is raised high and suspended in the air.[2]

Side by side, one angel is of ice, the other of fire: it was always assumed, of course, that there was some unfriendliness between them. But the rabbis, outraged by this idea, retorted that no insults were being exchanged—taking as their evidence the verse, 'he maketh peace in his high places'.[3] It would be quite wrong to spread such malicious gossip, they said: after all, weren't Michael and Gabriel together witnesses at the marriage of Adam and Eve?[4] Later at Messina, Omar would be vehement in his denial of this old rumour: 'They are not enemies, and you are mischievous asses.' They have been brothers in arms since the world began.

Michael does have an enemy, though. His very name denotes this, for in Hebrew 'Michael' means 'Who is like unto thee, O Lord?' This question sets him fiercely against the angel who has the blind vanity to reply, 'I am', and to claim to be the equal of his Creator: that angel is Satan. The Apocalypses, both Jewish and Christian, bear witness to the violence of their first battle, the day when Michael was charged with presenting Adam to the other angels, so that they would bow before this creature made in the image of God: this magnificent angel[5] refused. Michael immediately flew at him and drove the rebellious angel out of the heavenly court. Mad with rage, Satan tried to grab hold of Michael's wings and drag him down with him as he fell.[6]

So as enemy of the prosecutor of the human race, Michael is man's friend and advocate; until the end of time, it is he who will present and defend the souls of the righteous in

1 Meaning the 'divine presence of God'; in the Cabbala it refers to the tenth sefira, through which the flow of divine energy comes to Earth. Trans.
2 *Sayings of Rabbi Eliezer*, chs. 3 and 4.
3 Job xxv, 2.
4 *Genesis Rabbah* viii, 15.
5 Called Sammael in the Jewish versions.
6 *The Assumption of Moses*, X.

God's tribunal. Having a name in the form of a question repeated by Moses,[1] Michael is also quite naturally devoted to protecting the children of Israel, those great interrogators in the presence of the Eternal One. And it was Michael who rescued Abraham from Nimrod's furnace, who announced the birth of Isaac to Sarah, who fought with Jacob, blessed him and gave him the name of Israel, and instructed Moses in the Law.[2] After that, once there was a people, Michael— 'prince of Israel' and 'one of the chief princes', according to the faithful Gabriel's revelations to Daniel[3]—would uphold the house of Israel in all its battles, aided by some 4 billion 960 million angels who, under his orders,[4] formed an invisible and invincible army.

The Cabbalists, who symbolise God as ten divine emanations (*sephiroth*) corresponding to a human body, say that Michael was reared on the milk of the fourth, *hesed*—which means 'love', and is located in the right arm. Michael is powerful love.

The circumstances of the Koranic revelation and Michael's immense popularity among Jews have undoubtedly prevented him from making as brilliant a career in Islam as his colleague Gabriel (Jibrīl). Nevertheless, Mikā'il enjoys an impressive reputation there. Like Gabriel, he was one of the four archangels given the responsibility of carrying out God's wishes on Earth, and only He knows how many wings he has. If Mikā'il cannot now approach either heavenly or earthly creatures without consuming them in his light, he owes his rule of the winds, the tempests and the rains to his original, now forgotten, iciness.

Nothing, on the other hand, prevented Michael from making a career in Christianity—quite the opposite. 'It is he who was prince of the synagogue, but who is now established as prince of the Church,' said Jacob of Voragine in *The Golden Legend*. Wanting to be 'the new Israel' themselves,

---

1 Exodus xv, 11.
2 *Genesis Rabbah* xliv, 16; *Targum Genesis* xxxii, 25; *Deuteronomy Rabbah* xi, 6.
3 Daniel x, 13, 21.
4 A. Abecassis and G. Nataf, 'La Merkabah', in *Encyclopédie de la mystique juive* (Encyclopaedia of Jewish Mysticism), Berg.

Christians naturally adopted its guardian angel with his impressive biblical CV—heavenly warrior, friend of man, judge of souls and great vanquisher of the Devil. So we find him baptised as Saint Michael, archangel. Saint, and no half-measures, because Christian angels are either saints or devils and we know which side he is on—and with what determination he sticks to it! And archangel, because he commands legions of angels.

He will not take long to display his talents.

THE ARCHANGEL MICHAEL

Christianity's superhero

In spring 452 Attila arrived at the gates of Rome—with his hordes of Huns, as was his wont. Emperor and army had but one idea: to flee for their lives. The Romans, thus abandoned, turned to Pope Leo I who decided to try to persuade the barbarian, in exchange for a ransom, to leave Rome in peace. Forty-five years earlier Nicasius, Bishop of Rheims, had won the crown of martyrdom in this dangerous game. No matter, because Leo had an ace up his sleeve: before leaving, he solemnly consecrated the city of Rome to Saint Michael. And the miracle happened: Attila listened to the pope's reasoning and left, with all his Huns dutifully following behind him. Immediately a beautiful church was built in honour of the victorious archangel, and it would be dedicated to him the following 29 September, which became Saint Michael's Day.

In February 590, it was the turn of the plague to sweep through Rome; corpses were heaped alongside the dry river bed of the Tiber, and the air stank. Gregory the Great, Abbot of Saint Andrew's on the Caelian Hill, whom the Christians wanted to elect pope but who did not want the honour, after three days of general fasting had Saint Luke's portrait of the Virgin Mary brought out, and the Romans marched in procession behind it. At the head of the line, Gregory suddenly heard invisible voices singing from the other side of the river what would become 'Regina coeli'—'Queen of Heaven, rejoice, allelujah!': At the same time, he looked up and saw on the Castello of Crescentius, the emperor Hadrian's mausoleum, the archangel dressed as a warrior in the act of putting his bloody sword back into its scabbard. The air was suddenly pure: Saint Michael had conquered the plague. Gregory ended the heavenly hymn with a 'Pray to God for us!', before becoming pope, saint, then Doctor of the Church. The tower of the mausoleum, rebaptised 'Castel Sant' Angelo', acquired an immense statue of the glorious Michael, while he gained another feast day, 8 May.

But when it comes to giving the devil a good thrashing, Michael doesn't have to be asked twice. In the fifth century he had chosen the Monte Gargano in the kingdom of Naples as his chief sanctuary,[1] where he had exploded the infamous cult of the idol Mithras. In 706 he appeared to Aubert, Bishop of Avranches in the Cotentin region of Normandy. In his diocese loomed the frightening black forest of Scissy where sun worship still flourished, one of whose gods was Belenos, well known to readers of Astérix. All this was a headache for Aubert, in whose eyes these false pagan gods were truly Satan's henchmen.

So one night Saint Michael appeared to Aubert and asked him for a sanctuary on Mount Tombe (which dominates the region), like the one he already had on Monte Gargano. The next day the bishop, who was a down-to-earth sort of man, persuaded himself that he had dreamed it all and that his daytime worries must be invading his dreams. So he made himself forget them. Weeks passed, and suddenly the forgotten dream recurred, this time with Michael furious to see the bishop so little moved to obey him, for he wanted his sanctuary! The next day Aubert once again convinced himself, although it took some doing, that he had been hallucinating; he forced himself not to think about it again. When the archangel Michael appeared for the third time, he was beside himself with rage; he shook Aubert and, jabbing a finger at his head, declared that since he was so disbelieving he would leave him a sign. Waking with a start, Aubert had the distinct impression that something had drilled into his skull. However, there was nothing to be seen.

It was a long time before Aubert's skull could be examined.

1 Now known as Monte Sant' Angelo. Trans.

In fact, it was not until hundreds of years later, when Aubert had been canonised and his skull had been promoted to official relic, that a hole was found in it left by the angel's finger, similar to a hole made by a trepanation. Sufficient to say that even by the beginning of the twentieth century doctors still had not managed to explain this phenomenon. Sceptics are invited to go to Avranches in the Manche department, where they can visit the treasure of the Basilica of Saint Gervase, which keeps this perforated skull tied very elegantly with a piece of gold string.

Anyway, Aubert finally got the message. He started work on an underground basilica on Mount Tombe, similar to the one on Monte Gargano, where he sent two young monks to look for a piece of marble that Michael had trodden on (just as Gabriel had placed his hand on the rock at Jerusalem) along with a piece of the archangel's red mantle that he had left behind to decorate the altar. The monks' journey, from the Cotentin to southern Italy and back, would take two years. When they finally returned with their precious angelic relics, the forest of Scissy had disappeared and all that was to be seen on the shore was Mount Tombe. Six months earlier, in March 709, an earthquake accompanied by a tidal wave had made the coast crumble away into the sea. Called to his aid by Aubert, Saint Michael had saved the mountain, where every creature, even the wild animals, had taken refuge. Satanic idolatry had been swallowed up with the forest, and Lucifer had once more been defeated. Crowned by its abbey, Mount Tombe became the Mont-Saint-Michel, and the archangel earned himself another feast day, 16 October, which was added to the original Monte Gargano one of 17 November. So Michael has no less than four feast days all to himself.

It would have been churlish, of course, to neglect Monseigneur Saint Michel, the guardian archangel of France. In 710, Childebert III consecrated his kingdom to him. In 732, Charles the Hammer invoked him at Poitiers and the Saracens were defeated. In recognition of the heavenly reinforcement that Michael had brought him in his wars agains the Saxons, Charlemagne had no hesitation in changing the standards of the Franks into votive offerings—henceforth all were to depict the archangel, with this embroidered inscription: 'Behold, Michael, the great prince, has come to my aid.'[1] In 1214 Philip Augustus, who had been baptised in Saint Michael's Chapel in the Palais-Royal, Paris, also gained a famous victory at Bouvines, near Lille, thanks to his intervention. Would that they had begged for his help two centuries later at Agincourt, where the flower of French knighthood, bogged down in the mud, perished under the arrows of English archers. But let that pass, for never during the whole of the Hundred Years War—which in fact lasted 116[2]—was the Mont-Saint-Michel, though besieged, actually taken.

And guess whose voice it was, in the summer of 1425 when France was occupied, that came to whisper to the little Joan of Domrémy?[3] This is what she said at her trial:

'It was Saint Michael whom I saw before me, and he was not alone, but accompanied by angels from heaven ... I saw them with my very eyes, as well as I see you now; and when they left I wept, and wished that they would take me with them.'

'What doctrines did Saint Michael teach you?' [asked an interrogator.]

'Among other things, he told me to come to the aid of the King of France ... The angel told me of the desolation in the kingdom of France.'

Joan also predicted to her judges the following, which she would not see: 'Of the love or hatred that God has for the English and of what He does for their souls, I know nothing; but I do know that, except for those who die here, they will be hounded from France, and that God will send victory to the French against them.'

And so it was. To be fair, we should point out that if Saint Michael led Joan into battle, Gabriel visited her in prison, on 3 May 1431, where she said she had received 'the comfort

1 *Ecce Michael, Princeps magnus, venit in adjutorium mihi.*
2 Or a minimum of 138, if the Treaty of Picquigny of 1475 is taken into account.
3 Joan of Arc. Trans.

of Saint Gabriel'. Moreover, both archangels are depicted on her standard.

It was quite logical, then, that when Louis XI created the first royal order of knights he should put it under the banner of Saint Michael, 'the first knight to gain victory in battle, in God's cause, against mankind's old enemy and topple him from heaven, and who has always successfully protected, pre-served and defended his seat and oratory which is called Mont-Sainct-Michel; for never has it at any time been con-quered, nor fallen into the hands of our kingdom's old enemies'. The thirty-six knights of Saint Michel, chosen from among the bravest in Europe, were never to remove their gold neckchain, on which hung six shells and a medallion with his image.

Michael is still, in our time, serving in the French army—as patron saint of the parachutists. The idea originated in Free France's military training camps that were set up in England during the Second World War; for who better than Michael could have protected this new kind of flying warrior? Since then, the legionnaires of the Second Parachute Regiment have taken over the SS song invoking the devil and turned it into one proclaiming his conqueror: 'Not only have we arms, but Saint Michael, who marches with us!'

Gabriel, too, is in the French army—as patron saint of the Signal Corps. Also, since 1951 he has pursued a discreet but far-reaching career as head of the French postal and telecommunications service, in memory of the message that he once carried to Mary. In addition, the current development of the media is considerably extending his field of operations: at this very moment he is surfing the net!

The angel and the hermit

JEWS, CHRISTIANS OR MUSLIMS?

As natural travellers, angels fly unblinkered from one mono-theism to another.

Sometimes they leave behind some strange tales, which end up so similar that even the most eminent scholars have a hard time tracing their origin. 'The Angel and the Hermit' is undoubtedly the most widespread of these stories; it can be found in one form or another in the Babylonian Talmud, in the 'Lives of the Fathers' in the Koran, in the *Sefer Maasiot* of Rabbi Nissim Gaon, in a *Life of Merlin,* and even in Voltaire's *Zadig,* directly inspired by the Englishman Parnell.[1]

First, the seventh-century Christian version. A hermit in the Egyptian desert keeps begging God to reveal His judgements to him. One day, his prayers are answered: an angel appears to him in the guise of an old man, and asks him to follow him. So off they go. They arrive first at the home of a nice fellow who welcomes them and gives them everything he can. By way of thanks, the angel steals a dish from him. The man then sends his son after them to retrieve it. Without more ado, the angel throws the son down a precipice. They continue on their way and arrive at the house of an abbot, who refuses to let them in; in the end he allows them to stay in one of his stables but gives them nothing to eat or drink. However, the next day, the angel gives the abbot the stolen dish.

The hermit is shocked: are these really God's judgements? The angel then reveals the meaning of his scandalous behaviour: the dish was stolen in the first place, and it does not behove a virtuous man to harbour an object of doubtful provenance; on the other hand, an evil object was revisited on an evil abbot, thereby only accelerating his fall from grace. As for the good man's son, had the angel not killed him he would have assassinated his old father that very evening. That decent old man, so sorely tried on Earth, would now be able to enjoy eternal life to the full, while the evil abbot, who had been rewarded on Earth, would have nothing to lay claim to later and would go straight to hell.

The appalling injustice of this world is but an illusion; the reality is the justice of the next world, where God makes His most important judgements.

In the contemporary Muslim version,[2] Moses takes the place of the hermit and a holy man that of the angel. Moses,

---

1 Thomas Parnell (1679–1718), writer, Archdeacon of Clogher in Ireland and friend of Swift and Pope. Trans.
2 Koran xviii, 65–81.

then, meets a wise and holy man and asks if he can follow him in order to learn from him.

'If you are bent on following me, you must not question my judgement about anything until I mention it to you myself,' the wise stranger says to him. The two set out, but as soon as they embark on a boat, Moses' companion bores a hole in the bottom of it.

'A strange thing you have done,' Moses comments. 'Have you done it to drown the passengers?' The stranger reminds Moses that he has promised not to open his mouth. They continue on their way and encounter a young man. The stranger kills him.

'You have just killed an innocent man who has slain no one. Surely you have done a wicked thing?' The stranger once again reminds Moses of his promise, and Moses apologises again. They walk on together until they reach a town where they ask for some food, but the inhabitants refuse to receive them as guests. They come upon a wall there that is falling down, and the stranger restores it.

Moses says, 'You could have asked them to pay you for your labours.'

This time he has gone too far.

'The time has come for us to part,' says the other. 'But first I will explain to you those acts of mine which you did not have the patience to watch.

'You should know that the ship belonged to some poor fishermen. I damaged it because at their rear there was a king who was taking every ship by force.

'As for the youth, his parents both are true believers, and we feared lest he should plague them with wickedness and unbelief. It was our wish that their Lord should grant them another in his place, a son more righteous and more filial.

'As for the wall, it belonged to two orphan boys in the city whose father was an honest man. Beneath it their treasure is buried. Your Lord decreed, as a mercy from your Lord, that they should dig up their treasure when they grew to manhood. What I did was not done by my will. That is the meaning of what you could not bear to watch with patience.'

The meaning of this Koranic story is that men, who are short-sighted and quick to judge, are unable to grasp the harmony of God's plans. Only God is wise, good and just. Muslims recognise in the stranger the prophet Al-Khadir, who lives in eternity, beyond time and space, and appears sometimes to the chosen few. This form of angelic existence is not unlike Elijah's role in Jewish tradition. Furthermore, Muslims see the origin of this Koranic tale in the Jewish story of Elijah and Rabbi Joshua ben Levi, who lived in the third century.

The story is told by Rabbi Nissim Gaon in a collection that he wrote in Kairouan in the tenth century, to console his father-in-law Dunash on the death of his son. Rabbi Joshua, he writes, has fasted and prayed for a long time for God to send Elijah to him. When Elijah appears, Rabbi Joshua tells him that he would like to accompany him so that he can learn from him. Elijah replies that he could not manage such a journey. But as Rabbi Joshua protests, Elijah relents. He warns Rabbi Joshua, though, that at the first question from him he will leave him.

They set out. That evening they arrive at the house of a couple whose only possession is a cow. The husband and wife put their guests in their best room. The next day, Elijah prays and the cow dies.

'Why did you make the cow die, when this unfortunate couple received us so kindly?' Rabbi Joshua asks.

'If you want to leave, then I'll tell you,' Elijah replies.

So the Rabbi holds his tongue. The next day sees them at the house of a rich man who refuses them hospitality. Now, it so happens that a wall of his house is falling down; Elijah says a prayer and rebuilds it. Rabbi Joshua is dumbfounded, but somehow manages to keep his mouth shut. He suffers in silence, and walks on.

That evening they enter a great synagogue in which everyone has a seat made of gold and silver. The people there treat the travellers with contempt, giving them only water, bread and salt. And they have to sleep on the spot.

'May God make you all into leaders!' Elijah says to them as he and the rabbi leave the next morning. Rabbi Joshua finds it harder than ever to contain his distress.

In the evening they come to a new town, where everyone makes a fuss of them and pays them the greatest respects. The next day Elijah offers a prayer, then adds: 'May God give you only one leader!'

At this point the rabbi explodes and demands that Elijah explain everything to him.

'The man whose cow I killed,' the prophet explains, 'was to lose his wife that day: I asked God if the cow could serve as a ransom for her soul, for a woman is a great asset, and very useful in the house. The rich man whose wall I restored would have found a great treasure, had he dug out the foundations. And if I prayed to God to make all those men leaders, it's because it will be to their disadvantage, for so the proverb goes: "Too many pilots sink the ship." Finally, if I asked God for the others to have only one, it was for their own good, for, as the *Ben Sira*[1] has said, "With a single protector, a town will hold its own."'

Other than learning that women are worth more than cows—a truth of which urban intellectuals frequently tend to be unaware—the specialists conclude that, in writing this story, Rabbi Nissim was inspired more by the Koran than by the Talmud: for did he not live just after Mohammed, and in a Muslim country? He would have suppressed the murder of the young man so as not to upset even more his father-in-law, who was grieving for his son. In any case, the story in the Talmud[2] itself seems like a shortened version of a Jewish legend now lost for ever—and which, for all we know, could be the true source of all these stories.

Which came first? We no longer know, but it does not matter. What counts is that Jews, Christians and Muslims alike should have orchestrated these few notes carried on the wind in the night of time and made from them the eternal story of the angel who, in the face of man's wretchedness, defends God's honour.

We can see just how far the tale has travelled when Voltaire picks up the thread and puts his Zadig face to face with

---

1 Also called The Wisdom of Jesus the Son of Sirach, or Ecclesiasticus, and found in both the Jerusalem Bible and the Apocrypha.

2 It has Benaya, a son of the Sanhedrin, and Asmodeus, king of the devils.

an angel. But if, eleven centuries later, the story is exactly the same as in the old Christian tale, its conclusion is very different. Voltaire was neither Christian nor atheist, but a philosopher and a theist. The God in whom he believed was not the one who speaks in the Holy Scriptures, but the fruit of his reflections. So it is no longer a question of eternal life as justification for the angel's attitude, but one of simple morality. As for the dish, if the angel stole it it was because the man who had played the good host had only done so out of vanity; deprived of his dish, he would become a wiser man. And as for the beneficiary of the theft, he was a miser who would learn the benefits of hospitality through this gift. The universe is rational and justice immanent. The angel explains:

> '"There is no evil from which good is not born. There is no such thing as chance: everything is either trial or punishment, reward or providence. Poor mortal, stop fighting what you should be worshipping."
>
> "But," Zadig said . . .
>
> As he said the word "But", the angel flew off towards the tenth sphere.'

This angel, a disciple of Leibniz, knew neither sympathy nor compassion for the 'poor mortal' and wanted nothing to do with his objections—could not even be bothered to listen to them: the God of the philosophers, known as 'the clockmaker', the 'eternal geometrician' or 'the architect of the world', has lost the tender mercy of God the Father. In contrast to the God of Abraham, who always, in the end, yields to men's prayers, cries and even their attempts to bargain, this supreme being is a sort of general administrator, indifferent to the complaints of His subordinates.

So it is not surprising, given the way they portrayed Him, that within a century the philosophers had ditched this detestable God—one wonders whether he even merited a capital letter. He had the sort of face that deserved to be smacked. I hope we can be allowed to prefer God in His original version, along with Rabbi Nissim's comforting conclusion.

Before he left, Elijah added: 'Don't be surprised if you see a bad man content, and don't take offence, because his present happiness will be his ultimate misfortune. If you see a good man wretched and in trouble, suffering from hunger, thirst, destitution, don't be annoyed and don't commit the sin of doubting your Creator. Believe, rather, that God is just, that His judgement is just, that His eyes watch over the ways of man. And who will dare ask Him, "What are You doing?"'

With these words, they took leave of one another, and went their separate ways.[1]

Does this not show a true angelic gentleness?

---

1 From the Amsterdam edition of 1746.

Conclusion

In which the author ventures a few wishes that she hopes are not pie in the sky.

There are many other stories we could tell.

If there were a chapter called 'The Thriller', for example, how could we not mention Munkar and Nakīr? It would be wrong to leave out these two terrible Muslim angels, whose job it was to interrogate the inmates of the cemeteries. Scarcely had a man been buried, and with 'the crunch of his companions' footsteps still receding into the distance',[1] than our two villains would arrive. They would make the corpse sit up and then interrogate him on his faith. If he replied, 'I swear that there is only one God and that Mohammed is his prophet', his tomb would be 'enlarged by seventy cubits and filled with greenery until the day when all the world would be resurrected'. But if the defunct turned out to be an unbeliever or a hypocrite, Munkar and Nakīr would say to him, 'You know nothing, and you have read nothing!' and hit him between the ears with an iron club. The corpse would then cry out so piercingly that 'the whole neighbourhood, except for men and djinns, would hear him'. His tomb then shrank until its sides jammed together.

In certain regions of Anatolia they used to build very high tombs deliberately, so that the dead could sit up easily and welcome Munkar and Nakīr in a dignified manner. Popular tradition has it, thank God, that if the believer had not committed any sins he would be interrogated by Mubashshar

---

1 Bukhārī and Muslim.

141

and Bashir, two angels who were, apparently, completely charming.

Then, if there were an 'Animals' chapter, we would give some space to Grigio and mention that, according to a Muslim proverb, angels will not enter houses where there are dogs. However, all the biographers of Saint John Bosco pose serious questions about Grigio—an enormous and terrifying grey dog. He turned up mysteriously one November evening in 1854 at the priest's side while he was wandering, lost, through the more unsavoury suburbs of Turin, and guided him home. No one ever knew where he came from nor to whom he belonged. And it was not for want of searching. At moments of danger, if Don Bosco was under attack, he would suddenly appear from nowhere and accompany him back to his house. Then he might disappear for years. He was ferocious with villains but very gentle with children, and no one ever saw him eat or even accept the smallest titbit in the kitchen of the orphanage[1]—which was not very dog-like, any more than was his age, because in 1883 he seemed just as frisky and robust as when he had first appeared some twenty-nine years earlier. When interviewed, Don Bosco would say no more than that 'this dog was not like other dogs'.

What the saint did not dare say, 'because he didn't want people to laugh', was that his Grigio was an angel. However, ever since the time of the prophet Zechariah (about 520 BC) it has been known that there exist in the heavens 'red horses, speckled, and white' which 'the Lord hath sent to walk to and fro through the earth'[2] so that they can report to Him. All the commentaries stress that these talking horses who go off to inspect the world are angels. So angels can indeed adopt an animal form.

Even so, you cannot catch an angel in a butterfly net—and in fact myriads of them have passed through our ill-adapted meshes. How could it be otherwise? The traditions are numerous and the angels innumerable, and their story

---

1 John Bosco, the founder of the Salesian order, devoted much of his life to helping destitute young people.
2 Zechariah i, 8, 10.

began well before mankind's: it is difficult when one is not a poet to claim to have read every book on the subject.[1] By their very nature, the angels' archives seem destined to be skimmed.

And you do need to know when to go no further than the threshold of a mystery. Because, a million miles from esoteric spells, real secrets do exist—the kind a person glimpses when he or she sees the invisible. Unless she has been given a message, and generally a very short one, she cannot and will not talk about it. One of the most famous in this respect, Saint Teresa of Avila, would never have written a line about her experience had she not been forced to by her superiors. When God is looking for confidants, He does not choose chatterboxes. The friends of the Word are people of few words.

Also, true mystics have problems with words, which are simply inadequate to describe what they see; they keep emphasising the poverty of their vocabulary and their lack of knowledge when faced with what they need to describe. To follow them, to try to understand them, demands the spiritual commitment of a lifetime. There are only three mystics in each of the three religions who can open the debate at this level.

But would they do it? No, in all likelihood. At this level of consciousness, it is impossible to envisage any argument. Only unbelievers would try to win or be won over, both urges aroused by the same violent feelings; true believers, on the other hand, succeed in reconciling themselves through the singular relationship that they have with their Creator. In looking up to God, they are united, just as the angels are— without having to deny their identity, but rather by taking it to its extreme. Leon Askenazi said to a conference in 1968, jokingly: 'I was told about a miracle cure at Lourdes, that involved an apparition. And I believe it. That does not mean to say that Christianity is true. It just means that God takes care even of Christians.'

---

1 A reference to the nineteenth-century French poet Stéphane Mallarmé's famous line: 'La chair est triste, hélas! et j'ai lu tous les livres' (literally, 'The flesh is sad, alas, and I have read every book.') Trans.

No longer is it a question of arguing about God, but of sharing Him. Father Christian de Chergé wrote:

I am thinking about Sheikh Ishaq, who went to spend a few moments in silence at the tomb of a Muslim, while paying no attention to that of a Jew on the other side of the wall. That night he dreamt that a voice told him that he must also pray for the Jew. How is that possible? he asked his father, who offered him in reply a verse from the Koran: 'The believers are a band of brothers. Make peace among your brothers and fear God, so that you may be shown mercy.'[1] He then left to pray over the other man's tomb.[2]

The man who told this anecdote was the prior of the monastery of Tibhirine in Algeria; his fate was to be beheaded by fanatics along with six of his brother monks. In their memory, an enormous crowd of Jews, Christians, Muslims and men of goodwill gathered in front of the Trocadero in Paris and laid there a mountain of white flowers.

Ten years before, Father Christian had chosen this question of Julien Green's[3] as an epigraph to a meditation: 'When will religions at last become bonds between people, like hyphens between words, and stop being just additional reasons for killing one another?'

May the angels, those tireless weavers of invisible bonds, venture into the spaces between human beings. Forging links, after all, is their eternal role.

Ours is to follow them up the ladder that they set up one night while Jacob slept.

And at the very top we shall be with God.

---

1 Koran xlix, 10.
2 Christian de Chergé, *L'Invincible Espérance* (Invincible Hope), Bayard, Centurion.
3 Catholic novelist, dramatist and diarist (1900–1998).